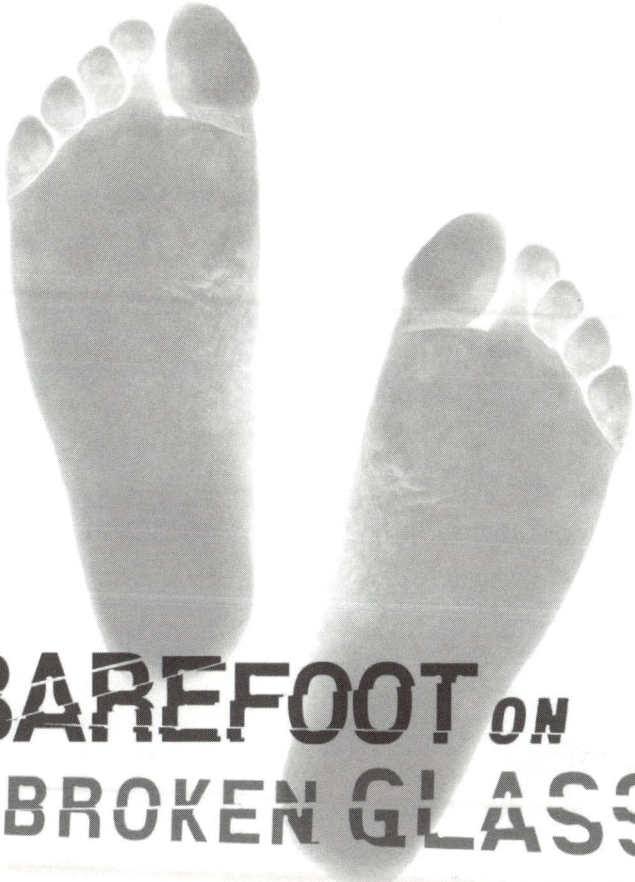

BAREFOOT ON BROKEN GLASS

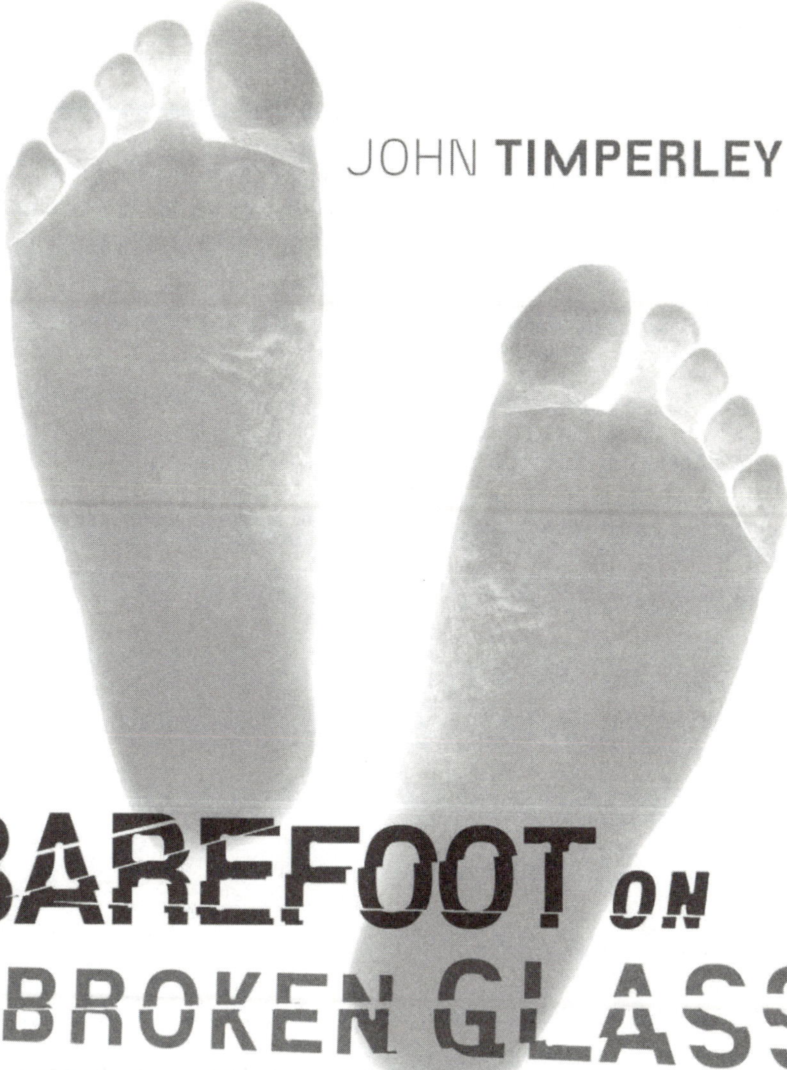

JOHN **TIMPERLEY**

BAREFOOT ON BROKEN GLASS

THE FIVE SECRETS OF PERSONAL SUCCESS IN A MASSIVELY CHANGING BUSINESS WORLD

CAPSTONE

First published 2000 by
Capstone Publishing Ltd
8 Newtec Place
Magdalen Road
Oxford OX4 1RE
United Kingdom
http://www.capstone.co.uk

Capstone US
Business Books Network
163 Central Avenue
Suite 2
Hopkins Professional Building
Dover
NH 03820
USA

British Library Cataloguing in Publication Data
A CIP catalogue record for this book is available from the British Library

ISBN 1-84112-1266

Typeset by
Forewords, Oxford
Printed and bound by
T.J. International Ltd, Padstow, Cornwall

This book is printed on acid-free paper

Contents

Acknowledgements

My thanks go to Mark Allin and Richard Burton of Capstone Publishing for believing in the concept, and me, and for the their advice which transformed a manuscript from what is was to what it has now become. Thanks also to my agent, Liz Puttick for doing her job so professionally and well, and to John Shango, who gave me the courage to walk barefoot on broken glass.

I am particularly grateful to my PricewaterhouseCoopers colleagues who have allowed me to gain a glimpse into the future for business and the people within it.

And last, but not least, I am especially indebted to all those 'great' people who have allowed me to use their words as quotations in this book. To encapsulate a big idea and give it life in a handful of words is the mark of a true master.

Dedication

To my wife Joanne and our three daughters, Melissa, Jessica and Hannah.

You are my inspiration and greatest teacher.

Barefoot on broken glass

That's a funny title . . . what's it all about?

When I first started this book I wanted to gather together what I thought were the very best and most inspirational lessons for personal development and apply them to today's business arena. Along the way I found huge similarities between what makes great organisations and great people 'tick'.

By the end of this book you will know about a set of personal skills that will allow you to achieve extraordinary results for yourself and your organisation.

You will be able to use this power, if you wish, to focus on what will bring you success, happiness and balance in a turbulent business world.

The secrets of personal and organisational success are in fact, identical. They are: adapt to, or create, change; ensure that your people's full potential is unleashed for the benefit of the business, create a believable vision and get them to focus on it with passion, commitment and a real sense of urgency.

That's not all, the great organisations of the new millennium help their employees cope with the demands of modern life and give them the tools to shape their own future success.

Barefoot on broken glass has five stages – five personal development secrets – which are set out in a logical and cohesive order. Having said that, the book has been designed so that each section can be read on its own, which means that you can jump about to your heart's content. All I would ask is that you eventually read them all – they are interlinked – and that if you *really* want to get full benefit, go back and re-read them in order.

Conscious that you want information, not guff, and 'do-able' action, not padding, the chapters have been created to be a short and pithy read. The first part of each is about you and your abilities and potential, and is wrapped up by a 'Bulletin Board' summary.

That's followed by a look at how the secret is applied to business, the real world of making money, serving people, becoming successful and outperforming the rest. And at the end of each chapter you'll find the five 'killer' questions to test your progress in transforming 'reading about it' into 'doing it.'

Along the way you'll find scores of quotes from 'great' people, some very current, others now long gone who, in a few poignant words, can often capture the essence of the 'secret' more successfully than a page of text.

> ***You can, indeed, walk barefoot on broken glass simply by adopting, and using, the secrets of success highlighted here.***
>
> ***But more importantly, you will also know the qualities which have made all great people and all great organisations great.***
>
> ***The material in here is just a taster to whet your appetite.***
>
> ***There's much more that could have been written – and you'll find it for free on the Barefoot website*** **www.barefootbook.com**
>
> ***Look out for the references as you read.***

As a marketing director with the world's largest professional services firm, PricewaterhouseCoopers, I have been in the enviable position of being involved in some of the changes affecting our clients and our own people, and this book mirrors that 'hands on' approach. *But I found that such experience was not nearly enough*; the words really had to come from the heart – from personal challenge.

Already an avid user of mind maps and other creativity techniques, and familiar with the daily challenge of setting targets, running meetings and managing priorities, these skills were already within my 'comfort zone'.

Time after time when analysing what made the great organisations and people 'tick' the same words kept coming back to me. They had focus – they knew what they wanted to do – and they backed it up by massive commitment. The 'greats' didn't stop until they achieved the results they wanted, and once they had achieved them the great organisations and people invariably set themselves a new challenge, recognising that there is no such thing as the 'finish line'.

So I resolved to put myself to the personal test by doing something that would stretch my comfort zone far beyond where it had been before; to recreate some of the heady mixture of excitement and fear experienced by the people and businesses you'll find throughout this book . . . so I taught myself to walk barefoot across twelve feet of broken glass.

There's no magic or trickery in it. The ingredients for the 'walk' are simply 2000 shards of glass and two bare feet. The secret of success? A focused mind, creativity, the willingness to have a go, and commitment to go through with it . . . all which you will learn here.

Walking on broken glass is a powerful physical metaphor for shattering the shackles of apprehension that grip all of us when we try anything we are unsure about. People who inspect the glass shards before I walk simply don't believe it can be done – and remain unconvinced until I step off the other end unscathed. (Have a look at the website video now at http://www.barefootbook.com and see the proof!).

You may not ever want to walk barefoot on broken glass, and I wouldn't blame you if you didn't, but the point is that you could if you really wanted to. I know from my own personal experience that you have a reservoir of latent potential inside you right now. All you have to do is tap into it.

And don't believe that this book is aimed at someone else: its message applies absolutely to you, whatever your circumstances or career path. Today's icons of success didn't all start out that way. But they were all unafraid to try, to risk failure and, indeed, to 'bomb' sometimes. Here's some examples of the early starts of some of our best, and most loved, organisations and folk.

- **Richard Branson** suffered from dyslexia as a child (and has managed to largely overcome it), was nearly expelled from school and left as soon as he was able. Mind you, he'd already set up a publishing business while he was there. His headmaster's parting comment was that 'Branson will either end up a millionaire or in prison.'
- **Bill Hewlett** and **Dave Packard** met on 23 August 1937 to discuss the founding of a new company. Did they have the great idea to revolutionise the way we use technology? Did they heck! They started the company first and then tried to figure out what they would make, moving forward and trying anything that might pay the bills. The computers came later.
- **Sony**'s early story was the same. When Masaro Ibuka founded the company he and his seven initial employees brainstormed what they would make. The resulting products could have been better. The first, a rice cooker, didn't work properly and Sony's first tape recorder failed in the market.
- **Pete Waterman**, of pop music team Stock Aitken Waterman fame, the creator of massive worldwide hits in the 1980s, couldn't read until he was in his twenties (dyslexia again). It didn't stop him becoming a multi-millionaire.
- **Walt Disney**'s first cartoon series *Alice in Cartoon Land* was dubbed by the critics as a 'limp, dull and largely cliché ridden enterprise.' It flopped.
- **J. Willard Marriott** started out selling root beer from a market stall.

- **Boeing**'s first aeroplane failed, and the company had such a hard time making ends meet in the early years that it moved into the furniture production business to remain solvent!
- **John Mills**, the legendary British actor, always knew he wanted to be on the stage. But it took him three years to save up £14 from his job in a corn merchants before escaping to London . . . to find that the only work he could get was as a toilet paper salesman. He was a dismal failure and was sacked. Success only came along when he was 'discovered' by Noel Coward a couple of years later – in the Far East of all places.

The point is that 'greatness' can come to anybody, to any team, if you know how to create it. Contrary to popular belief, personal and business success doesn't always fit neatly into a business school case study. The people and organisations featured here succeeded (are succeeding) because they tapped into their potential and were unafraid to try new things and 'have a go'.

I've included stories from people I admire, and case studies from organisations, some 'blue chip', and others that have the potential to be the 'shooting stars' of the future. All have actually gone out there and done it. I hope you find it a potent cocktail of ideas and inspiration.

I hope you take many things from this book. I hope the hundreds of examples and quotes will stimulate you to take action for yourself and your organisation and that some of the ideas will take root in your mind. But above all I hope you take with you the confidence and inspiration that this stuff does work. You *can* learn the techniques of 'the greats'. You *can* apply them. You *can* become whatever you commit to be.

If you have any comments or questions on any aspect of the book, drop me an e-mail at capstone_publishing@msn.com.

Introduction

Scientists have proved that most of us use less than 1% of our brain's potential. That leaves an awful lot of spare capacity, no matter how intelligent or creative we are at present. This book shows you how to utilise more profitably the tools you already possess in order to:

- Think faster and more creatively
- Do more in less time
- Identify and achieve your goals in your career and life
- Remember more and absorb information faster
- Strengthen your power to get things done
- Use your thoughts to balance your life

People these days are starved of time and overloaded with too much work. Today long hours at the office are not just for workaholics, they have become the norm. And as competition intensifies there appears little relief in sight.

This is the book you will need in an age when the pace of change has never been faster, where pressure to perform has never been greater, and where stress-related illnesses have rocketed to levels which have shocked the medical profession. Running away from change or trying to slow it down is not an option, the momentum is far too great. The healthy – and only – alternative available to us is to use our own untapped capabilities to equip ourselves to meet the personal and organisational challenges affecting us now.

As with any adversity there are people and organisations who are thriving. They've learned do more and make a bigger impact, and to release time to achieve their goals.

All of the skills in this book, although necessary for success, were probably never taught to you in school and are rarely taught on the job. By using your mind in a more productive and creative way you can perform at a higher level than ever before.

The key theme throughout these pages is that the prize goes to activists; the people and organisations who use what they know to achieve results. Often they are not the smartest or most sophisticated; they are people and businesses who are simply unafraid to try new approaches to make more of themselves and squeeze the most our of their business and personal lives.

The question is, what do you want? Try this quick exercise to guide your thinking:

Tick those feelings, abilities and 'things' you want more of, and then in the second column rate your top ten in order of importance. What do the answers tell you about where you are now and your hopes for what your future could be like if you got what you wanted?

What do you want more of?	Tick here	My top 10
'Success'		
Time to do things		
Respect		
Love		
Ability to do what I want		
Appreciation		
Fun!		
Energy		
Fitness		

Health		
Responsibility		
Self confidence		
Opportunity		
Money		
Family life		
Challenge		
Certainty		
Direction		

The ideas and exercises in this book can help you to get more of what you want. They are based on six key principles:

- **Getting the most out of life involves overcoming obstacles and challenges**, both personal and organisational. Dealing with them, not avoiding or resisting them, is the mark of the successful
- **Victims don't exist**. You have choices; you are not a victim of circumstances without your own permission. You have the ability right now to do what you want in life and your business, and to make decisions that will lead you to more success than you have at present.
- **You are already successful**. You have latent abilities just waiting to be tapped into. Even if you have already achieved a great deal, you can easily do so much more if your desire to 'have a go' at new things is strong enough.
- **What you know counts for nothing unless you do something with it**. You've got to act on your knowledge and skills. Knowledge without action is useless. Action is the key to taking life, and business, by the scruff of the neck…and loving it.
- **It's not about you, it's about your contribution**. We can build on our strengths and minimise our weaknesses so that we can give more to our loved ones, our employer, friends . . . the world – and boy does the world need your contribution!

- **Now is the time to do it!** The momentum of change today is immense, and change brings opportunity . . . if you view it that way.

The thoughts presented here are relevant to all of us, but in different degrees. If one particular aspect feels distinctly uncomfortable to you, look again. The most uncomfortable is very often the thing we need to do to learn and grow – it is the edge of our comfort zone. And the more we visit it the more familiar the landscape becomes. Come on, let's make a start.

"Tomorrow's leaders will have to learn how to create a environment that actually embraces change, not as a threat but as an opportunity"
Warren Bennis

Secret 1

Change to survive and thrive

"We've got to learn to live with chaos and uncertainty, to try to be comfortable with it, and not to look for certainty where we won't get it"
Charles Handy

Chapter 1

Embrace the pace

In this chapter . . .

- **Learn to ride the wave of change**
- **Handle the stressful emotions created by change**
- **Adopt four positive mindsets to help you thrive on change**

There are three key drivers of change impacting on all of us right now; the world population growth, massive advances in technology and the explosion of easily accessible information.

Today there are more people in the world than ever before. In the 1860's the world population was 1bn. It doubled in 75 years to 2bn. It doubled again in the 50 years to 1975, and today it stands at 6bn. In the year 2080 we are forecast to have 10bn people on the planet. More people bring with them more ideas and better, cheaper and faster ways of doing things. In short, they create more competition.

> ***"The world is moving so fast these days that the man who says it can't be done is generally interrupted by someone doing it"***
> Harry Emerson Fosdick

The world has also become a smaller, more uniform and sophisticated place through technology. Eighty per cent of all inventions and technological advances have been made since 1900. And with more people developing and using technology further rapid change is inevitable. There was more information created in the 30-year period between 1965 and 1995 than in the 5000 years before. This volume is doubling every five years, and it's readily accessible almost everywhere in the world through the advent of the Internet and other global forms of communication.

The 'global village' first conceived by Marshall McLuhan in the 1960's has become a reality for many millions of people exposed to CNN broadcasts, MTV and America on Line. Never before have we been able to communicate so easily with each other, regardless of distance.

More information going to more people faster than ever before means more chances for *change*; change means doing new things, or doing old things in a new way, but will almost always take us to our limits. It can, if not handled properly, cause stress. And, as someone once said *"If you're not riding the wave of change … you'll find yourself beneath it."*

- How big is the wave? Here's an inkling:
- All of the world's manufacturing output in 1949 is now produced in a single day
- All of the world's scientific projects carried out in 1960 (including the major Apollo and Russian Cosmos space initiatives) are now carried out in a single day.
- All of the phone calls made in the world during 1983 are now made in one day.
- Not surprisingly, all of the e-mails sent in the world in 1990 are now despatched in less than 24 hours.

Quite staggering statistics, but probably nothing when compared to the speed of change we will see over the next five years. The spread of computer viruses drives this message well and truly home. It takes only six hours for the latest virus to get right round the world. Computer boffins have now calculated that if an initial 30 people contacted another 30 people on the web, and so on, we're only six clicks away from reaching the entire planet. Whew!

Peter Cochrane, British Telecommunications' Chief 'futurist' says that never before has technology allowed us to communicate with so many, so fast and so simply. "Life," he argues "is going to get much faster. We'll know more faster, and we'll have to make decisions faster. The information explosion literally is 'chaotic' in the true mathematical sense."

There can be no slowing down or stopping, the momentum of technological advancement has already been created. The secret to coping is adaptability; we need new moves, not old reactions. However, our basic instincts of 'fight or flight' often take us over. We decide, consciously or not, to fight the new ways of doing things, or to flee them and become a 'stress refugee'. But there are fewer and fewer places to run – the whole world is changing, not just your own life.

> ***"There is no security on this earth, there is only opportunity"***
> General Macarthur

Luckily, we all have the personal tools and the power to turn change to our advantage. This book will give you the techniques to make full use of your innate abilities.

To feel in control of our lives we need to understand our emotions and how they control our attitudes, thoughts and actions. The knack is to choose the 'best' emotion for a situation and the 'best' attitudes, thoughts and actions follow on naturally. But first a quick self-test.

How *comfortable* are you with these situations?	Very	OK	Oh no!	Aargh!
An increase in your responsibility by 50%				
Change of job				
Change of boss				
Move to another city to work				
Having to make your people redundant				
Having to learn new personal and technical skills				
A 25% increase in your workload				
A move into a totally new market sector				

A role which involves you being a spokesperson for your organisation or work area				
Your competitor has just taken 20% of your market share				
You are asked to lead your organisation/team to achieve a 20% annual increase in profit (or other measure if yours is a not for profit environment)				
You fall out with your partner/loved ones				
Your work colleague gets promoted ahead of you				

The trick is not necessarily to aim to be 'very comfortable' with all these situations. It is to recognise those which land heavily at the 'aargh' end of your comfort 'Richter scale' and to consider if the discomfort is holding you back and limiting your options for growth. Does the pattern tell you anything about your ability to adapt to aspects of change in your personal or professional life?

Let's explore some very familiar attitudes and then revisit them from a different viewpoint.

Expect someone else to reduce the pressure on you

Let's be honest, we generally don't like change in the workplace. We were happy before the companies merged, before the computer got even more complicated and before we had to read twice as many e-mails. It was much easier when we didn't have to do twice as much work, before we had to work in a different location and so on. Whatever the change is, we often perceive it to have resulted in more 'pressure'.

We spend our days blaming the top management, the economic situation, customer demands, competition, market shifts or new technology. And we can dissipate our precious time and energy blaming something or somebody for our situation. Because 'somebody else' has caused this change and increase in pressure, we believe that somebody else will have to reduce it.

In entertaining these thoughts we become the 'victim'. Subconsciously we believe that people will help us because we feel sorry for ourselves. In reality, all we do is load ourselves down with self-inflicted stress and set ourselves up for future victimisation.

> ***"Change is not achieved without inconvenience, even from worse to better"***
> Richard Hooker
> 16th century

+ The survival kit

Make the conscious decision to stop blaming everyone and everything for how you feel. Accept responsibility for your own emotions. Whatever the cause, change is a continual evolution in which we are all involved. Note how you are feeling in a certain situation and if it is uncomfortable, explore the reasons.

Decide not to change

Some of us resist change either at work or home, and fight it out in the open or by stealth. Either way it's a tough emotional battle. Organisations and people *have* to change to survive, it's always been that way. We often waste far more energy clinging onto old beliefs and ways of doing things than it would take to adopt new ones.

If your organisation or environment is changing, it's your wake up call to change also. Our work habits need to reflect the new demands on us and our organisation. Struggling to do things in ways which aren't now effective is like travelling at 80mph in second gear; it's a rough ride and immensely wearing on the system.

> ***"When faced with the choice between changing and proving there's no need to do so, most people get busy on the proof"***
> John Kenneth Galbraith

✚ The survival kit

We do have a choice in how we react to change. Our own attitude to a situation dictates whether we feel excited or threatened by the challenges we face. The key is to study how the game has changed, to identify our new priorities, and to wholeheartedly immerse ourselves in those areas where we can get the greatest return for our efforts.

Aim for a more comfortable pace of change

Many of us long for a more relaxed approach, a slower pace of change and less pressure to perform; the only problem is that this nirvana doesn't exist anymore. If we are changing we'll feel the stress of change – but if we are not changing we will soon feel even more pressure.

Those competitors who have grasped the nettle earlier will now be better, faster or cheaper than we are. The gap will have widened and, guess what, we'll need to change at an even greater pace to close it or risk the consequences of failure.

> ***"The difference between champions and the rest is that the champions amongst us never lose the killer instinct.***
> ***No matter how good we become, we mustn't be complacent"***
> Mark McCormack

Some of us try to find a balance to this by choosing a pace of change we are comfortable with. We rationalise that we can minimise the pain of change by pacing ourselves. But this can be a dangerous delusion if our own 'comfortable' pace is less than that required by our organisation or our relationships. We rationalise that we can minimise the pain of change by pacing ourselves. But this can be a dangerous delusion if our own 'comfortable' pace is less than that required by our organisation or our relationships. We risk being left behind – and 'tail-enders' almost never complete the race.

+ The survival kit

Very few low stress organisations are on track to survive. Those who are making successful progress have taken the decision to endure the trials and tribulations of change. Don't let your mind fool you that it is OK to take it at whatever pace fits your comfort zone. Keep to the speed set by those leading the way. Focus on tangible actions and techniques to maximise your personal productivity.

Attempt to control things you can't influence

We worry when we feel we have no control over what is happening to us – and the more we feel like we're losing control the more we struggle to restore our influence and balance. Many times, however, we simply do not have the mental or physical ability to affect the situation; we are trying to control that which is not ours to control. This feeling is the stuff nervous breakdowns are made of; at the very least it's mentally draining and causes us unnecessary suffering.

> ***"Instead of seeing the rug being pulled from under us, we can learn to dance on a shifting carpet"***
> Thomas F. Crum

+ The survival kit

We all need to accept some things as they are by observing our situation and asking ourselves if, realistically, we can really influence the outcome. If the answer is 'no' then we should decide to move on and concentrate on areas where positive action can make a difference. This avoids the constant churning of thoughts of what has happened to us in the past, or what is likely to become of us in the future. By keeping focused on what we can personally influence we avoid the feeling of paralysis, which is often the soul mate of change.

Bulletin Board

Change is inevitable and will be a constant feature of all of our lives. The quickening pace of innovation means that the only practical approach is to adopt attitudes and emotions that welcome change and help us to positively adapt to, and thrive on, new ways of doing things both in our work and social lives.

The alternative, resistance, can cause nothing other than friction and stress.

Business sense

Commentators recognise that there are several powerful, and sometimes hugely conflicting, forces at play in business today. Whilst the trend towards globalisation is increasing the dominance of the multinational players, internet-based organisations and niche businesses can mop up market share because they are agile and innovative.

> ***"The best of everything always survives"***
> Richard Branson

Industries are now entering each others' markets – witness the retailers closing in on financial services (the Marks & Spencer charge card, Virgin financial products, etc) with the net result being fierce competition and significant pressure on prices . . . and people.

Add to that the demands of both institutional and private investors for quick (and substantial) returns and you have the most competitive environment in the history of commerce.

But, paradoxically, the increasingly complex, technology driven world could be making the search for elusive success factors easier because the management gurus believe that people – motivated, creative and flexible people – are what will ultimately make the difference. Systems won't do it, marketing strategies won't either, but people with imagination and conviction will.

Gary Hamel describes it this way: "Never has it been so difficult to sustain success. Previously if you missed it by a year you could catch up. Now you'll never catch up. Sustaining performance whilst recognising the tremendous impact of changing technology, economics and markets is, ultimately, the province of *people* working in or with organisations."

The fact is that your attitude can be *the* critical factor in your success, no matter what your skills.

"Compaq employees know that individual and collective success can only continue if they embrace change as an opportunity, rather than reacting to it in crisis mode"
Eckhard Pfeiffer
CEO, Compaq Computer Corp.

Tom Peters tells the wonderful story about Southwest Airlines. It goes like this . . . Upon walking into the company's Dallas headquarters a prospective 'new hire' pilot was not as pleasant as he might have been to the receptionist, not realising that she had a potentially decisive role in his subsequent hiring. When the company chose not to offer him a job, Chief Executive Officer Herb Kelleher commented 'there are a lot of people who can fly airplanes, not so many with great attitudes'.

By the way, how's yours?

The five 'killer' questions

Am I . . . ?	Yes	No	Maybe
Expecting someone else to reduce the pressure on me?			
Deciding not to change (when I really should) in aspects of my work and social life?			
Hankering after a more comfortable pace of change?			
Trying to control things that I can't influence?			
Running away (mentally) from any situations I should face?			
What am I going to do next?			

Do your answers reveal anything that strikes a chord? It's easy to 'tick the box', but harder to do something about your situation, particularly if the action to be taken is uncomfortable. We all need a way to stretch our own 'comfort zone' so that it becomes easier to make the changes we want. Let's find out how . . .

Chapter 2

Stretch that comfort zone

In this chapter . . .

- **Overcome the straitjacket of your own comfort zone**
- **How to set goals to reach your dreams**
- **Learn to create a success mindset**

Some people habitually look at new ways of doing things. These 'initiators' have broken free of the programming of our education system with its 'right or wrong' answers and learned how to use their mistakes as feedback to enable them to grow. They use the experience to develop new and better ways of doing things and don't get hung up on being labelled 'wrong'. In short, they are happy stretching their comfort zone.

> ***"Minds, like bodies, will often fall into a pimpled, ill conditioned state from mere excess of comfort"***
> Charles Dickens

The comfort zone is our personal area of thoughts and actions within which we feel comfortable. It is all the things we have done often enough to feel comfortable doing. Anything new is outside the comfort zone and, well, feels uncomfortable. As we'll see in these pages, our natural instinct is to gravitate towards comfort.

We see 'uncomfortable' as a sufficient reason for not doing something.

We know when we are at the perimeter of our comfort zone because we feel frightened, angry, guilty, unworthy or hurt – most of which leads to discouragement. And discouragement, as we all know, stops us doing what we are doing.

Our comfort zone can plague our lives and limit our ability to reach our goals. The bad news about the 'zone' is that it is never static. It is either expanding or contracting, and if you're not actively expanding yours, it contracts. It tends to hit us at our weakest point and comes in the form of reasons or excuses why we can't do the thing that is making us uncomfortable.

The key is to use the emotional energy created when your comfort zone is threatened and turn it into energy you can use to meet challenges and do the things you are called upon to do. In fact, as we'll discover, many people don't have any goals simply because the mere thought gets their comfort zone playing up.

"You gain strength, courage and confidence by every experience in which you really stop to look fear in the face. You are able to say to yourself 'I lived through this horror – I can take the next thing that comes along'. You must do the thing you cannot do"
Eleanor Roosevelt

People who do overcome their fears, write down their goals and make them clear, vivid and measurable are, in fact, many times more likely to achieve success in life than those who don't.

A study of Yale University final year students way back in 1953 revealed that only 3% of them had written down their goals. Twenty years later the university attempted to track down all the former students who took part in the initial research, to understand what had happened to them in their lives.

The results were mind blowing. The 3% who had written down their goals in 1953 were tremendously more successful than the average, not just financially, but in their business, social and family lives too. They had achieved what they wanted.

The evidence from this and later research is clear, writing down your goals forms a mental and physical commitment to the direction you wish to go. It shows that you mean business and are not just dreaming wistfully about creating the life you want.

If you don't know what your goals are, or should be, the section on goal setting will help you. But before we launch into it, a few thoughts on mindset and comfort zone. Life is sweet and sour for all of us, and we have the opportunity to learn from our experience all of the time. But some of us try to make it as predictable as possible, and in so doing we considerably shrink our comfort zone so that we only attempt what we know we can do, or feel comfortable doing.

> ***"Unless you try to do something beyond what you already can do you will never grow"***
> Sir Winston Churchill

The 'Breakthrough' mindset, on the other hand, is one of accepting and dealing with challenges and obstacles, not fearing and avoiding them. Success is a journey, not a destination, and today's successful people are right now doing the things they need to do to move forward. They are taking calculated risks, paying attention to where they are now and where they want to be, and working persistently and optimistically to jump the fences along the way. That's the simple recipe for success.

If the thought of success and what you need to do to achieve it scares you a bit, take comfort in the words of Jan Carlzon who turned Scandinavian Air Service (SAS) airlines from an average carrier into a world class 'wow this is great' airline. He said (I paraphrase) "Instead of striving to be 100% better at one thing, try to be 1% better at 100 things."

> ***"You can't discover new oceans unless you have the courage to lose sight of the shore"***
> Ferdinand Magellan

Could you be 1% better at everything you do? Jan Carlzon transformed his organisation and made millions applying the concept. How about you?

Bulletin Board

Taking too much notice of your comfort zone is a killer – it kills passion, desire and the motivation to fulfil our dreams. Whilst it is there to protect us from what we perceive as harmful and uncomfortable thoughts and feelings, we must stretch it if it isn't to rule our lives. Taking action is the key; action designed to help us to move towards our goals. Successful people recognise that the comfort zone is ever present, but they work with it. So can you.

Business sense

There may well be several organisations that are over a century old – Philips, Ford, Mercedes and GE to name but a few – but the list lulls you into a false sense of continuity and stability. Take a closer look at their products and services and you'll see massive change – with many the name is perhaps the only constant. The facts show that the Fortune 500 churns around 30% of its members every seven years. These once BIG organisations are no more, taken over or merged perhaps, or fallen from grace. Every case tells its own story but the harsh business reality is that their position is filled with other dynamic, innovative businesses. Nothing stands still, and the best organisations are those that recognise the threat.

> *"My philosophy is that not only are you responsible for your life, but doing the best you can at this moment puts you in the best place for the next"*
> Oprah Winfrey

Take Boeing, for example, they developed a video for their people in the form of a future news report which highlighted the dramatic decline of the company. The idea was to theatrically hit home with the message that the company needed to change or face the future consequences. Stirring stuff – and a great way to get the emotion of the message across. Somehow I don't think a memo would have done it

The five 'killer' questions

Am I . . . ?	Yes	No	Maybe
Stretching my comfort zone enough every day?			
Clear about my goals for the next: month 3 months 6 months year 5 years			
Aware of the challenges I'll need to face or get round?			
Passionate enough about what I want to do?			
Willing to have 'good tries' and fail sometimes?			
What am I going to do next?			

Why not look on the Barefoot website at www.barefootbook.com for some great (and easy to use) templates to help you to think about your own goals, what they could be, and how you intend to get there. Treat it as good fun, not a chore, otherwise you won't implement the actions needed and you'll end up disappointed. The secret is not to focus on where you are now, but on where you want to be. All you need to do is to point yourself in the right direction and release your potential. The next section will give you an armful of ideas.

Where are you now?

You'll lay the foundation for personal success by wholeheartedly embracing Success Secret No. 1: you've got to change to survive and thrive.

Darwin said it, and so too does every business guru. Changing, of course, means stretching your comfort zone. Doing things differently, or doing completely different things adds up to increased pressure.

Predictions of what's going to happen in the future, and how fast it's all going to take place, abound. Once you recognise that change will be massive, and universal, and that you can't control it all, you can get on with the job of making the most of your own abilities and situation.

Let's start by understanding the secret of becoming more creative, soaking up information faster than you've ever done before, and being hugely better at retaining it all.

Barefoot on broken glass

To walk the glass requires a fundamental mind-set shift from "I can't do this" to "I can". It means confronting your comfort zone, suspending your disbelief and trusting in your ability to meet the challenge . . . creating, in fact, the attitude which is the hallmark of great people in all walks of life.

If you haven't seen it yet, visit the barefoot website **www.barefootbook.com** *to see how it's done.*

Secret 2

Release your potential

'The existing hierarchy in most organisations is a hierarchy of experience, not of imagination. And there is a big difference between experience and imagination.

Never has experience been worth less, and never has imagination been more central to future success'
Gary Hamel

Chapter 3

Awaken your creative genius

In this chapter . . .

- **Learn to be more creative than ever before**
- **Discover eleven ways to add the 'genius factor' to your work**
- **Use six approaches to crack tough problems**

Nothing happens until someone has an idea, and tests it to see if it works. Creating more and better ideas is essential if we are to respond positively to change. The more practical ideas we have the more valuable we are to ourselves, our employer, our family and friends.

> ***What we can see is only a small piece of the jigsaw. Creativity is having the vision to see the bigger picture.***

Some of us, however, find it difficult to be creative. We've lost the gift we had as a child of naturally generating a string of free flowing great ideas to meet the challenges we face.

As we become more logical, through our education, we tend to lose our lateral thinking ability. Whilst we can come up with the obvious solutions, we struggle to get the really creative ideas out. We've constructed a mental straitjacket for ourselves but,

"Innovation is not just about microchips and technology – it's about being new. New attitudes and new behaviour can be just as effective in the marketplace"
Barry Gibbons
Chairman and CEO
Burger King

fortunately, there are many easy to adopt tools to loosen its grip and let the innovative 'gems' flow again.

Our most important attribute is self-confidence – the inner belief that we can find a solution to a problem or create a previously unseen opportunity. Tests with hypnotism have proved that those given the trance suggestion that they were 'exceptionally creative' massively outperformed their creative results before hypnosis.

But we don't need hypnotism to gain improved results; we can do it ourselves by simply imagining that we are such a creative genius, a Leonardo da Vinci or an Albert Einstein perhaps. How would they approach the problem or opportunity? Literally put yourself in their shoes in your imagination . . . it works! Relax, play with ideas, even ludicrous ones, not all of them have to lead somewhere, or be 'logical'. Don't stifle the thoughts; simply discard those ideas you have no immediate purpose for at the end of your thinking session.

"A mind once stretched by a new idea never regains its original dimensions"
Oliver Wendell Holmes

Try some of these techniques to awaken the creative genius within you.

- **Listen to your subconscious**, your 'inner voice' (your intuition) often provides the answer if you take the trouble to hear it. That's what Einstein and da Vinci did. Write down any thoughts straightaway though, otherwise they'll disappear as quickly as they came. Why not start an ideas notebook? Richard Branson is one who swears by them, going through between six and nine hardback A4 notebooks a year, capturing his thoughts, impressions, ideas and observations at every opportunity – and it's not done him any harm!
- **Change your perspective**, by arguing the other side to your own

view. Play Devil's advocate ... what does the fresh look tell you? What would your competitor think of your new product, for example? How would they react . . . what would they do next etc?

- **Draw or doodle to get your creative juices going**. Or even write with your other hand, it helps you to create different brain connections through its novelty value. Pretend you are back at school. Go on, have fun!
- **Never accept the first or most obvious answer**. Ask 'what else' or 'that's good but what's better?' Looking for the second or third right answers will help your creativity to rocket.
- **Keep a pad handy** for capturing thoughts, especially at night. Dreams and half wakefulness are great spawning grounds for ideas.
- **Remove the penalty for failure**, applaud or even celebrate good tries! Make failure a learning process not a frightening or career threatening one. The healthy attitude should be 'OK, that didn't work, so what would?'
- **Increase 'fast failures'**. The sooner you can identify that something isn't going to work you can stop and try a new way. Do mini experiments, pilot exercises and straw poll research to minimise risk and get a quick impression of whether an approach is a runner or not.
- **Look out for killer phrases** like 'it won't work' or 'we've tried it before' or 'no one is doing it like this'. They are all dampeners on a good idea; see them for what they are.
- **Use the 'ready, *fire*, aim approach** to idea generation by getting as many ideas out as you possibly can. Don't be embarrassed by the mixed quality, really fire them out. Select the best from the comfort of your armchair afterwards!
- **Define the conventional first.** Many

> ***"Failure is our most important product. Companies must accept failed experiments as part of their progress"***
> R. W. Johnson Jr
> Johnson & Johnson

> ***"The innovator has for enemies all those who have done well under the old, and lukewarm defenders in those who may do well under the new"***
> Machiavelli

challenges have an obvious solution. Advertising agency creative teams often get the obvious approach down on paper first before letting rip with 'off the wall' ideas which may lead to a much more innovative solution. Getting the obvious answer in the bag helps clear their minds and gives licence for fresh and better ideas.

- **Change hats**. What does the situation look like from a different point of view – your client's, your partner's, the finance dept, production etc? Put someone else's hat on and see how they would view the problem and its potential solutions.

Use creative thinking to solve thorny problems

Ask questions to uncover solutions

> ***"In the middle of difficulty lies opportunity"***
> Albert Einstein

Philosopher Jonas Salk once said that the answer to problems already exists . . . to find it all we have to do is ask the right questions. For some issues asking questions is the best way to unlock your creativity and 'reveal' the answer. Try these – they will particularly appeal to the more analytical amongst us:

The analytical approach

To really get to the root of a problem ask:

- **What** is the problem?
- **Where** does it happen?
- **Why** does it happen?
- **When** does it happen?
- **How** does it happen?
- **Who** causes it, and who does it happen to?

The answers allow us to view the problem from all sides and give us an insight into the nature of the issue rather than some woolly feeling that something needs to be put right.

Let's take a quick example.

The problem is that our profits have been down for two months in a row. Something is amiss, but what? The analytical approach goes something like this . . .

Where?	Profits are down in our key product area, industrial paints
Why?	A competitor has just launched a new rival product
When?	The profit dip has been seen for the last two months – but what's to stop its further decline, given the competitor's new product?
How?	The competitor has undertaken heavy promotion for the new entrant, together with a low introductory price.
Who?	The competitor is No. 2 in the industry (we are No. 1). If the promotion continues we will lose market share, and so will other players.

"Innovation simply means that, whatever their job is, an organisation's people see their role as not just to be doing things the way they are designed today, but to figure out the way they ought to be done tomorrow"
John Kotter

Clearly, there are many other who, what, why, where, when and how questions that could be asked here to get to the root of the problem. But even in this basic example you get a feel for the nature of the issue and are probably already thinking of solutions and approaches that will get you back on top.

Ask 'dumb' questions

Asking 'dumb' questions gets us thinking and challenges our assumptions. Good examples include:

- Why do we do it this way?

"When you ask a simple question you get a smart answer"
Aristotle

- Who reads the information we provide, and what do they do with it?
- Why are we structured like this?
- Why do we need . . . ?
- And the final cover all . . . why do we do the things we do?

The answers can lead to fundamental changes when we recognise that we've done things through habit, for a reason which is no longer valid, or because someone in the past decided that was the way it should be done.

Curiosity is the beginning of success

Ask 'why?' five times

At Toyota they have a discipline of repeating the question 'why?' to get to deeper levels and find the real cause of a problem. For example:

1. *Why* has the machine stopped?
   A fuse blew because of an overload
2. *Why* was there an overload?
   There wasn't enough lubrication for the bearings
3. *Why* wasn't there enough lubrication?
   The pump wasn't pumping enough
4. *Why* wasn't enough lubricant being pumped?
   The pump shaft was vibrating as a result of abrasion
5. *Why* was there abrasion?
   There was no filter, which allowed chips of material to get into the pump. Installation of a filter solves the problem.

If we don't get to the root of the problem it will never be truly fixed, all we will succeed in doing is treating the symptoms.

Ask 'what if?'

Asking a 'what if?' question allows us to speculate and experiment. For example:

- What if we did it like this?
- What would happen if . . . ?
- What if we could produce for 10% less?
- What if members of our team were encouraged to ask 'what if?' questions all the time, what would happen?
- What if we could serve our customers twice as fast?

That's exactly the question the fast film processing companies have grappled with. It wasn't too long ago when 24 hour film turn-around on your holiday snaps was the best you could get. Then it moved to 2 hours. Now the latest one I saw was just 20 minutes.

These organisations have asked themselves what the impact on their competitive position would be if they processed films quicker than anyone else. The answer, judging by the fact that they are introducing shorter and shorter working times, is that they will win more customers – the impatient ones like me who are willing to pay premium prices to get my amateur efforts into my hands as quickly as possible.

Picture the future

What would the situation look like if the problem were solved? What would we be doing? Conjuring up this image often leads us to see the steps needed to achieve our vision of the future.

Our habits and ways of thinking in the business and home environment can create a mental straitjacket that restrains our creativity. All of us have the ability within us; it just needs to be cultivated. Creativity is like a muscle, if we don't use it its strength dwindles through inactivity.

> ***"To quadruple our profit we must double our failure rate"***
> Tom Watson
> IBM

Bulletin Board

Creativity is often no more than finding a better way of doing things – to do them faster, more efficiently, with more fun etc. When great thoughts and ideas come capture them fast, and watch out for those killer phrases like 'It'll never work' which can snuff out a brilliant idea at birth. Use the techniques you feel most comfortable with and vary them to suit the problem at hand. The key is to use them, as knowledge is useless without action.

Generate as many ideas as you can, and select those you can work with, rather than wait forlornly for the 'big idea' to come along. Remember ready . . . fire . . . aim.

Business sense

Art Fry's inspiration for Post-it Notes began when he sang in his church choir in the early 1970s, using scraps of paper to mark his place in the hymnal. Unfortunately, as you would expect, they kept falling out. 'I needed a bookmark that would stay put, yet could be easily removed without damaging the book,' he said. At the same time his colleague Dr Spencer Silver was working on adhesives research at 3M's research labs. He had just developed an adhesive that stuck lightly to many surfaces but remained tacky even after it was repositioned.

> *"The true capital of success and growth is not cash. The real currency of growth today is good ideas backed by great applications"*
> Jay Abraham

The rest is history, of course, Fry applied some to the edge of a piece of paper and his hymnal marker was created. More importantly, when he wrote a note on one of the pieces of paper and attached it to a report to one of his colleagues the feedback soon told him that the Post-it Note, a new way of communicating and organising information, was born. A deceptively simple idea, the Post-it Note has had profound business consequences for 3M, and the world wouldn't be the same without it.

But be warned, Post-its had their detractors. When they first saw them some people were appalled (what a waste of money) others thought them silly, some didn't know what to do with them.

The key question is, what would have happened if Fry and Silver had listened to them?

William E. Boeing, founder of the Boeing Aircraft company knew a bit about the dangers of listening to those who have a dampening effect on a new idea. 'It behoves no one,' he said, 'to dismiss any novel idea with the statement 'it can't be done'. Our job is to keep everlastingly at research and experiment . . . to let no improvement in flying and flying equipment to pass us by.'

British Telecom's Chief 'futurist' Peter Cochrane, sounds a strident warning to those organisations that won't or can't develop a creativity culture:

> "I see companies in danger of dying because they don't see the threat. Tired leadership, management, people, products and ideas sound the death knell. Experience, which once counted for so much, is only relevant in a world that isn't moving very fast. I don't know such a place."

> ***"The only sustainable competitive advantage comes from out-innovating the competition"***
> James Morse

Creating an organisation culture where creativity, new ideas and 'innovation' can thrive is certainly the challenge for business in the new millennium. But is not new. In the late 1920s arch-innovator Walt Disney paid his creative staff more than he paid himself. Disney recognised the business value of great ideas and the people who spawn them.

How do you and your organisation fare in the idea generation stakes? Try this quick litmus test to get a sense of your position in the race for new and better ways of doing things.

Do you, for example:

- Look for the areas where innovation can transform your business or sector?
- Pursue the 'open' management style so critical to the successful nurturing of new ideas?

"Incrementalism is innovation's worst enemy"
Nicholas Negroponte

- Push these views and raise the expectations and ambitions of those who will deliver the necessary changes?
- Know how new ideas are nurtured and harvested in your organisation?
- Make all knowledge created within your organisation freely available?
- Challenge the leaders within your business on how they behave towards, and support, new ideas and creative people?

"Vision is the art of seeing the invisible"
Jonathan Swift

The following chapters in this section on the theme of 'releasing your potential' highlight specific techniques to delve into your innate creativity (don't worry it's in there just waiting to get out) and how you can capture – and retain – information at a level you thought was only for the mega-brainy. Not so. Have a go!

But before that, try this . . .

The five 'killer' questions

Am I . . . ?	Yes	No	Maybe
Creative?			
Confident in my ability to come up with new ideas?			
Using all the different ways to be innovative?			
Encouraging colleagues and team members to do the same?			
Implementing the best ideas – even in the face of scepticism?			
What am I going to do next?			

There's no doubt that you can be massively more creative than you are now, not just for the sake of it, but with the purpose of developing practical ideas and innovative solutions to problems. The more you build creative techniques into your normal way of doing things the more you will use them automatically. Take 'mind-mapping' for example . . .

"When in doubt make a fool of yourself. There is a microscopically thin line between being brilliantly creative and acting like the most gigantic idiot on earth.

Chapter 4

Unleash your power to innovate with mind maps

In this chapter . . .

- **Discover mind-mapping, the brain's own way to record, retain, and create and innovate**
- **How to save hours note taking – and have more fun!**
- **Create your own maps to release your power to innovate**

Problem solving, opportunity spotting and the ability to see the 'big picture' are vital business and life skills. But once again, our schooling has not helped us to fully 'mine' our natural ability to collect essential information and use it. As soon as we are asked to capture thoughts, ideas or new information, almost all of us dive for a piece of paper and a pen and rush headlong into taking notes for fear of missing something – and we take notes exactly as we were taught in school, in a linear fashion, line by line until we've filled the page.

> ***"Any act becomes creative when the doer cares about doing it right or better"***
> John Updike

The huge problem with this is that it's not

the natural way the brain, or memory, works. Linear notes are a slow and massively inefficient way of collecting information and generating ideas. The brain works in pictures, not sentences. We need a method of capturing information in a way the brain relishes. Mind-mapping satisfies our brain's craving for something a whole lot more palatable and, frankly, more exciting!

Mind-mapping is a technique created by brilliant Mensa guru Tony Buzan. It's a tremendously enjoyable and effective way to accelerate your ability to record, remember and use facts and ideas. Learning and idea generation come easily, because the brain simply loves mind-mapping's use of colours, symbols, word and idea associations. It stimulates our intuitive right brain and gives our logical left brain something to get it's teeth into by seeing – on the page – links which may not have been clear in normal notes.

The great thing about mind maps is that they can be used by anyone of any age (young children are great at them because they are not locked into the restricted traditional learning approaches). Mind maps are like finding a key to your previously unopened door to creativity and innovation. A mind map is, after all, a type of sophisticated 'doodle' – something you would do when you are relaxed and your thoughts are flowing freely . . . the ideal mental state for creativity.

> ***"Our circuits are so overloaded by the technology that keeps us wired – the cell phones, modems and fax machines – that we've lost the capacity to doodle and daydream"***
> James Atlas

Here's how to get started. The 'mind mapper' shuns starting at the top of the page and working down in the note taking style passed down for generation to generation. Instead he begins slap bang in the middle with a word, symbol or idea and starts to branch out from there, adding ideas and facts as they flow, to form a tree-like structure with branches.

Throwing in colours and pictures as well as words, the mapper connects ideas, emphasises key points and highlights relationships that he feels are important.

Look at this to get the 'feel' of how a mind map builds up. The

The birth of a mind map

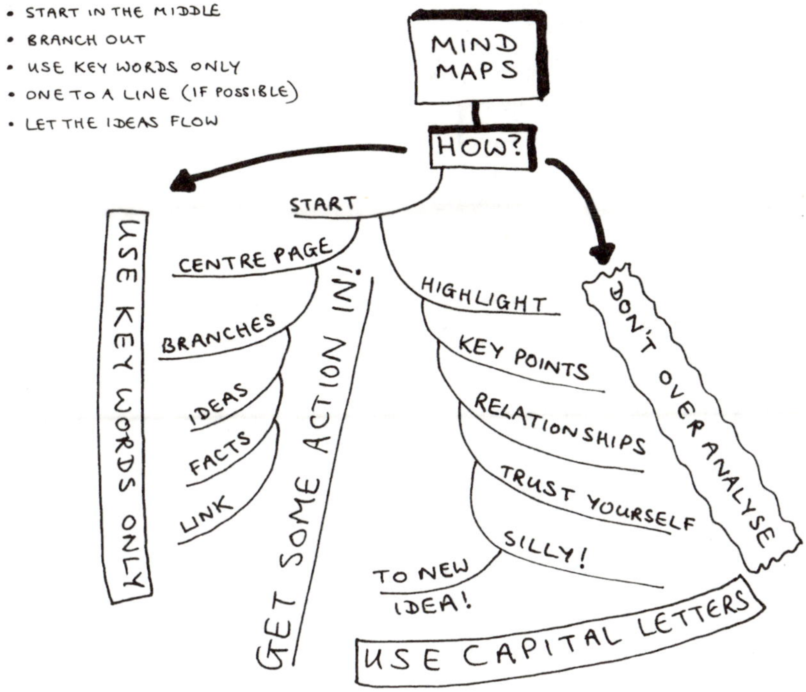

instructions on how to build your own follow on page **00**. When you've finished this section come back to the final map and see if it doesn't immediately allow you to review all we have said about the role and value of mind maps . . . in half a page!

The aim is to get all the branches of your mind map onto a single page so that you can see the subject and all its related facets in one go. This has five enormous advantages over the usual note-taking style.

1. The main theme is right in the middle of the page, and the importance of each idea relating to it is clear – the most vital will be nearer the centre, with sub-sets going outwards towards the edge of the page.
2. You can link concepts and ideas on the page. These are likely

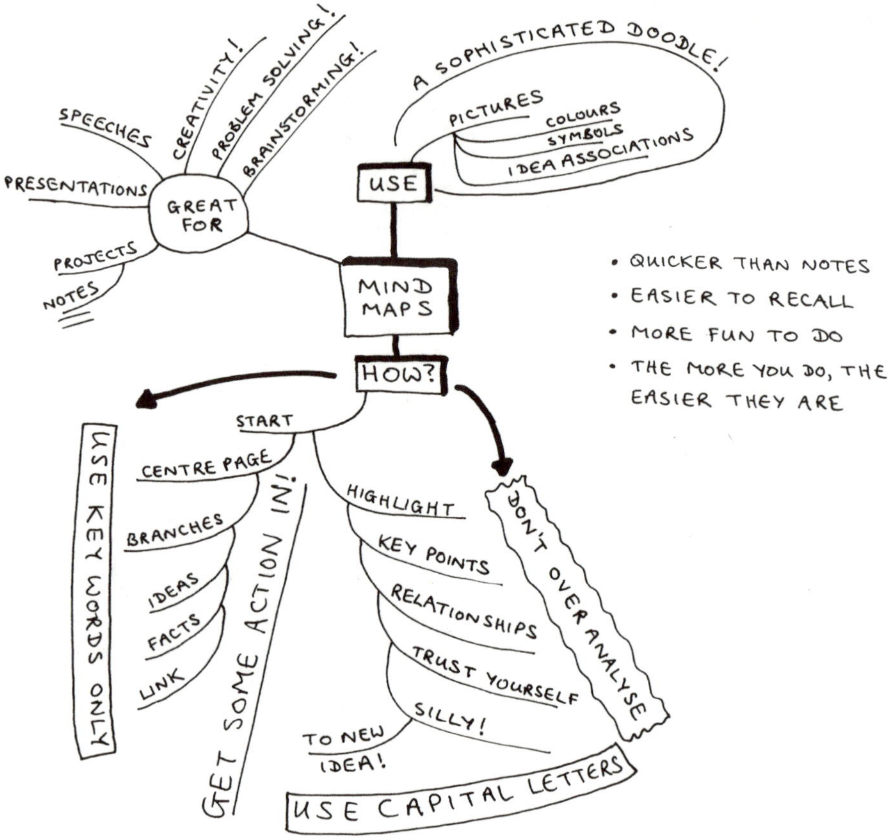

to be close together anyway because that's how your brain works, by associating one thought with another.

3. It's simple to add new information and ideas on a map because it is so flexible, unlike traditional notes on a page
4. Mind maps are much quicker and easier to create than long hand notes because they use single 'key' words
5. Each map is different because it depends on the connections your brain makes with new and already learned knowledge, and because they are unique they are much easier to remember.

Take a few minutes now to create your own mind map based on the

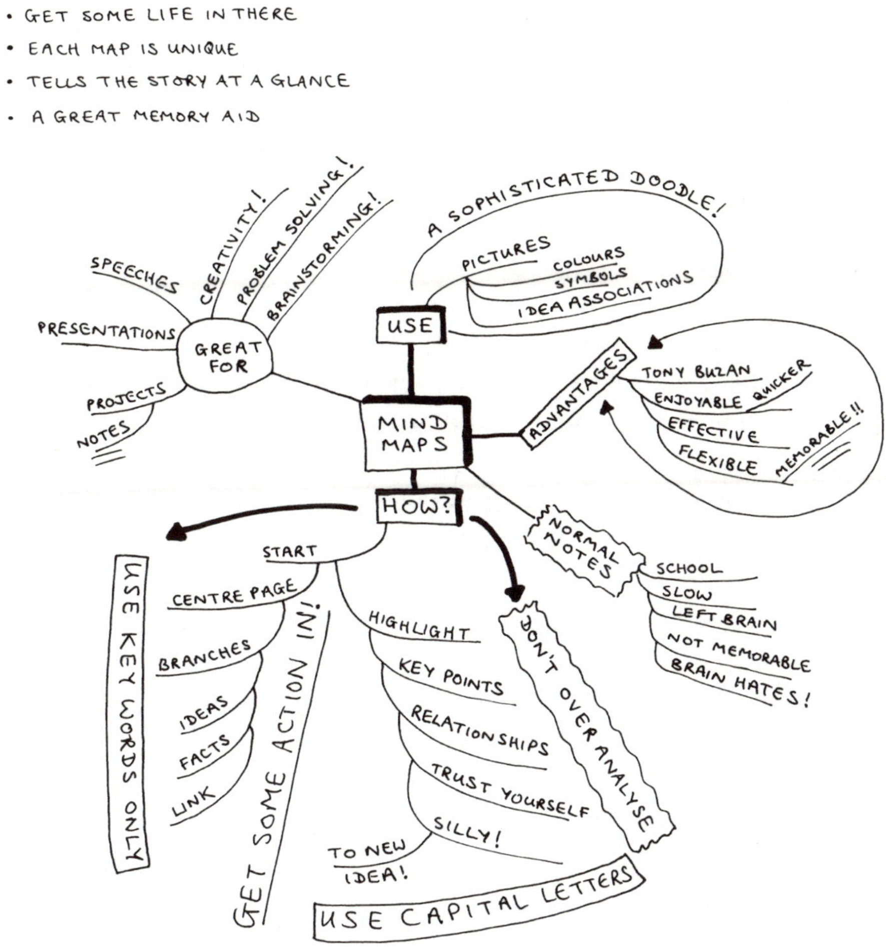

content of this section, using these pointers along the way. Feel how easy it is to create, and imagine how, with a little practice, mind maps could become second nature. Those who make a habit of using them would never do anything else.

> ***"What is now proved was once only imagined"***
> William Blake

A few tips:

- Print key words in capitals – your thoughts will come so fast your writing will be difficult to read otherwise.

- Each word or phrase should be on a different line, and each line connected to other lines. These are the basic building blocks of your structure.
- Keep to one word per line if you can (you don't really need any more) the word itself will prompt your recall.
- Go with the flow . . . use the key words, lines and tree structure as your tools and get your thoughts out onto the paper. Don't over analyse or over structure – there's plenty of time for that later if you really feel the need.
- Trust the links suggested by your brain, especially in creative or problem solving mode. Mind-mapping is a lateral thinking tool, and some of the links you make may be illogical, not relevant or even crazy, but don't edit as you go – the silly idea may be the one that works, or it could provide a stepping stone to a more practical one.
- Get some life and action into your maps. Just as memory gets a powerful shot in the arm through the introduction of ridiculous, unusual and out of proportion images, the same goes for mind maps. Make yours a work of art if you want to, but make sure that you get arrows, shapes and colour in there because the mind 'sees' in pictures not words.

Look at the example on page 43 and get a feel for this simple but so powerful technique. It covers the key areas of this book.

Use mind maps for . . .

Meetings and seminars

Capturing the essence of the information and comment at these events is crucial to squeezing the most out of them. Writing reams of notes is not only boring and takes your eye off the proceedings, your scribblings are a real disincentive to review . . . and most people don't ever refer back to their notes anyway!

Wouldn't it be far more enjoyable to do a mind map whilst you

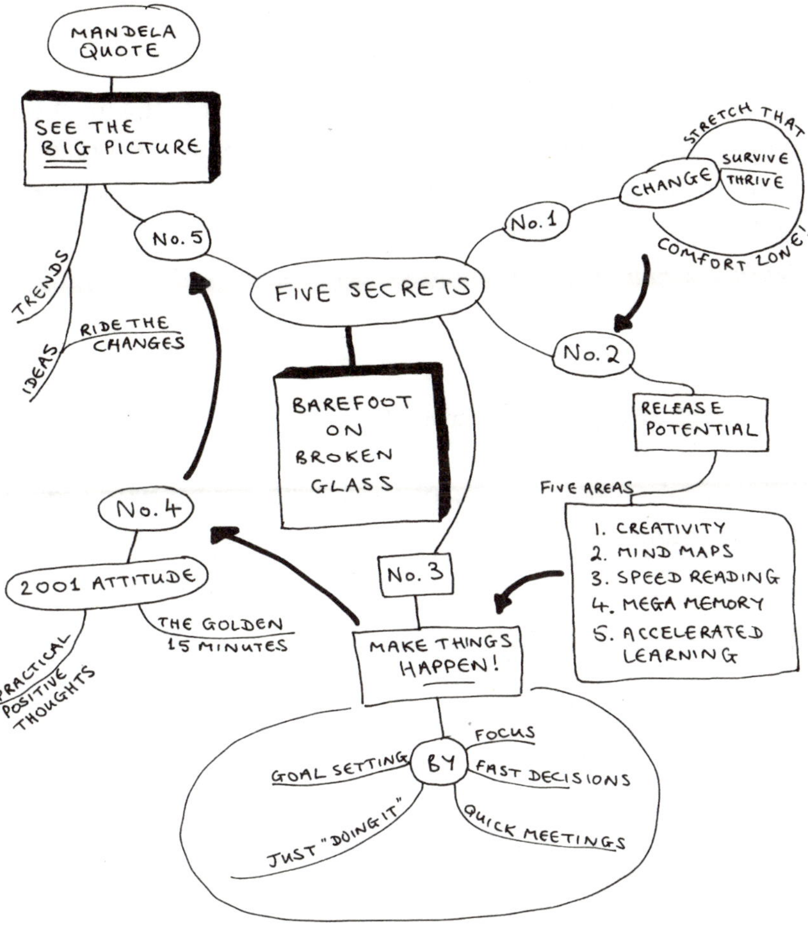

are listening, highlighting the key themes and action points, in a style that you can review very quickly and then decide what action you wish to take?

Project planning

Reject the linear approach and use mind maps for a change. The maps allow your thoughts to run free, you can see the interrelationships of tasks, ideas, people and so on, all of which can be brought together in a formal timetable later when you've explored all of the angles.

Presentations and speeches

Creating a theme and supporting material is often the most difficult part of any presentation or speech. Try using a mind map to first 'brainstorm' the ideas you want to get across, your key messages and facts, and relate them all to your audiences' needs. In next to no time you'll find that you have a strong basis from which to build a pithy presentation.

Creating and problem solving

When you've used mind maps to 'doodle' your way to great ideas and solutions you'll never revert back to a linear approach!

Brainstorm in groups

Because mind maps are quick and visual they are ideal to develop on a flipchart using ideas thrown in by your team. You can put everyone's ideas down on the same sheet so that all feel included.

Don't assess the merits of the ideas until the end. The 'off the wall' idea may contain the seeds of a great one!

Bulletin Board

Mind maps are not a wacky approach for odd people. Scientists have now proved that our brain works this way and, who knows, in the not too distant future our children may be taught this method as a matter of course, just as their parents were brought up on the traditional note taking techniques.

Make up for lost time and use mind-mapping as part of your daily routine now. It is an enjoyable and highly practical way of recording information, planning and creating. Stand out from the crowd by using mind maps to gain an edge.

Business sense

Ask any Chief Executive if he or she would like their organisation to be more innovative and the answer is likely to be a resounding 'Yes!'. But this is as far as some get. They assume that creativity and innovation is exclusively the preserve of small or high-tech companies, and that they are simply too big, or in the wrong sector, to innovate. This corporate mindset, coupled with inertia, blocks any further action.

> ***"Our company has, indeed, stumbled onto some of its new products. But never forget that you can only stumble if you are moving"***
> Richard P Carlton
> Former CEO
> 3M Corporation

They know they need to change, but don't know how . . . and they don't fancy failing. So the status quo remains. The trouble is that the organisations that have the courage to innovate can forge a 'never to be closed' yawning gap between themselves and their less creative competitors.

Worldwide research by management consultants at PricewaterhouseCoopers in 1999 showed that top innovators can generate over 75% of their revenue from products and services that were not in existence five years ago. For the poorest performers in the survey the figure was 10% or less – now that's a yawning chasm. What's the difference? What is it that makes some companies and people highly creative innovators whilst others stand on the sidelines wide-eyed in amazement?

This is what the top performers did: They made innovation a top priority at *board level,* and released risk capital to support bold ideas whenever and wherever it was needed. They constantly examined and re-examined where they should focus innovation efforts for maximum benefit and, what's more, the researchers saw that the people in these organisations were passionate about what they do and how they do it.

> ***"The ability to innovate, to learn and change is the hallmark of lasting corporate success"***
> Professor Mark Brown
> Director of Innovation,
> Henley Management
> College

The really interesting thing is that the highest performing and innovative companies came from diverse sectors. No, creativity isn't just reserved for the dot.coms, the biotechs, and the science parks – anyone can do it!

The five 'killer' questions

Am I . . . ?	Yes	No	Maybe
Using mind maps to unlock my creativity?			
Sharing the principles with others?			
Finding them easier to use than normal notes?			
Acting on the creativity generated?			
Feeling embarrassed about using mind maps 'openly' in my work?			
What am I going to do next?			

Trying anything new is awkward at first, and it's very easy to discard a good technique too soon as 'not being right for you'. I've found mind-mapping to be a fantastic help to me. Experiment with it for a while. It's one way to save precious time. So too is digesting the mountain of reading matter we all get on a daily basis. Here's how . . .

Chapter 5

Read twice as fast and retain more

In this chapter . . .

- **Double your reading speed with simple techniques**
- **Dramatically increase your concentration span**
- **Discover six ways to become a 'speed reader'**

You've got to read faster if you're going to survive in the corporate world of the future. No matter how fast you are now, it's almost certainly not enough to meet the demands of the information explosion.

> ***The speed of the leader determines the pace of the team***

Fifteen years ago business was conducted at a snail's pace compared to today. In those days secretaries opened the mail in the morning, bosses read and actioned it, and urgent responses were posted that evening to reach their destination the following day. The Royal Mail was king, and for most organisations it was rare for another document to arrive after the morning post had been opened.

Cut to the present, where we are bombarded with information through e-mail, faxes, the internet, the proliferation of new magazines and newsletters and, yes, the good old mail delivery which (for most of us) has slipped somewhat down the pecking order of preferred routes of providing information.

It's now much easier to send e-mail around the world than it is to post a letter. Indeed, in some organisations the number of e-mails you receive in a day has become somewhat of a status symbol. How many of us have heard the lament 'I've only been away two days and look, I've got 53 new e-mails' (with the unspoken comment being I must be one of the busiest/important/ interesting people in our area or business).

As communication has become much easier, the volume of information we receive, or need to have access to, has grown exponentially. Forget hankering back to the slower days of the past – they've gone forever. Forget also about blaming people for the proliferation of 'junk' information, because that's unlikely to stop too.

People all over the world are demanding more and better sources of information to enable them to make business and social decisions . . . and we're all drowning in the results of our own demands. If you are a business manager the latest research says that you may spend as much as 30% of your time reading reports, letters, faxes, memos, trade literature, newspapers, on line databases etc. That's an awful lot of time simply taking in information, with no immediate outputs as a result.

Luckily, reading a large volume of material quickly and accurately enough to make competent business and social decisions is within the grasp of all of us. There are two keys to cutting our reading time in half. The first is obvious, but often overlooked, choose *carefully* what to read. The second is something we are all capable of doing – we can train ourselves to read twice as fast as we do now.

You're probably 'coasting' as you read this. Your brain can process at 1000 words a minute but, if you're like most of us, you'll be travelling at 250–300, and you'll only retain 10% of what you've read after 36 hours.

With this sobering thought in mind, taking the first key first, the best piece of advice you will ever receive is 'don't read it'. Ruthlessness in what you choose to read is vital. For those items that do pass your 'Do I need to read this?' test make this your habit . . . skim read in a systematic way by focusing on the introduction, contents page, headings, anything in bold, and any summaries or publisher's blurb. Underline anything that is important.

Doing this at your normal pace will often provide enough information for you to decide whether it is worth reading further. If you really are going to use what you have read – and do something with it – sum up in your own mind (or on paper) what the key messages are, and criticise them if you have a different viewpoint.

Most important of all, write down what you are going to do as a result of absorbing the new information. This really is reading for a purpose. For most of us reading is 80% 'information in' with no real output to show for it – what a waste! All the knowledge in the world is of no use unless we do something with it and, what's even worse, in a few short days you will have forgotten nearly all of what you have read unless you take steps to retain it!

Now what about that reading faster stuff? There's no mystery to it. With practice you can read at least twice as fast as you do now, and at the same time carve out a huge chunk of free time in your schedule.

Part of the reason we are slow readers is that most of us read using only the left hemisphere of the brain, which tackles words in an analytical, literal and linear way. Our 'right brain' on the other hand is concerned with symbolic and spatial understanding and can comprehend metaphorical and intuitive meaning. So what? Well, if we can get both working together it becomes possible to understand text and read at phenomenal speed.

Speed reading using both the right and left hemispheres was developed from work carried out by US neuroscientist Diane Alexander while she was researching brain-injured children in California during the 1980s. Children who had suffered left hemisphere injuries which deprived them of speech were able to shift the verbal function to the right hemisphere and learn to speak again. Some of these children then began to read at incredible speeds using the right hemisphere.

In another experiment Manya and Eric de Leeuw measured a group of ten psychiatrists' reading speeds before training at an average of 334 words per minute (wpm). After training they had nearly doubled it to 647 wpm.

What's more, the psychiatrists began with a 78% comprehension of the text they were reading and, at the end of their training (even with their faster reading speed) they had increased their comprehension to 85%. Reading faster improves comprehension because the reader concentrates on the meanings given by text and is reading more actively.

The way we all learned to read at school, looking at each word and 'sub vocalising' it in our head, is largely to blame for our slow reading. To go faster we need to train ourselves to do three things, none of which are difficult. They are to stop less, move our eyes faster over the page, and to increase the number of words taken in at one go.

We can soon get used to missing non-essential words and looking for ideas and thoughts rather than individual words. The eye can see up to six words in one glance, and can move from one group of words to another four times every second.

Try this . . . ask your partner to hold a book up and begin to read. Position yourself so that you can see his/her eyes, and notice that the eyes move in small jerks, not smoothly along the lines of text as you might have expected. This is because the eye takes in blocks of words.

The only difference between fast and slow readers is that slow readers look at each word, may go back and re-read, and even look away from the text from time to time. Faster readers also have jerky eye movements but they jump longer distances by seeing groups of words, not single ones, and they don't go back to re-read either.

If you do sub-vocalise (say the words in your head) it is impossible to read faster than 300 words a minute. It's important then that your reading is entirely silent and visual if you wish to reach your potential.

Use these techniques to dramatically increase your reading speed . . .

1. If you want to read faster, just do it! The act alone of pushing yourself to quicken up will build your speed and concentration.

> ***We are what we repeatedly do. Excellence then is not an act, but a habit***

2. Train yourself to see more words at each glance. Divide sentences up into 'sense groups' of two to four words (see the example below). Practice reading the 'sense' groups, not the individual words. You'll soon get your brain used to the new technique if you practice for short periods over a week or two. Do the same by marking up passages in a magazine or book.
3. Also practice taking in blocks of words by holding the first two fingers of your right hand out, like a pair of dividers, and placing them randomly on a page to 'take in' four word blocks. Try to get the sense of the blocks at a single glance. This is a great exercise for really strengthening your concentration and your mental capacity to take in more than one word.
4. Work with your partner by asking him (her) to show you three or four words quickly (like a 'flash card') and then cover the words. What were they? Your ability to see them will increase dramatically, and so will your reading speed and comprehension.
5. Sounds a bit basic, but using your finger as a guide can really help you to stop less, prevent you going back to re-read, and helps your concentration immensely. Use your finger to increase your speed!
6. 'Go like lightening' by reading four or five pages as quickly as you can. Don't

> ***We learn our limits by going beyond them***

worry about comprehension. Then read the same pages at your 'normal' speed and you'll find you are considerably faster. It's the same effect you feel after driving on the motorway for some time. When you join the normal road network again 30 mph feels painfully slow because your mindset and reactions have been geared to a higher rate of travel.

Check your present speed by reading normally for one minute then count the number of words. Test yourself every day after you've practised the above techniques for just 15 minutes. In a month you'll have witnessed a tremendous improvement, in two months even more. It really is worth the effort to save so much of your valuable time.

Just a final word on the uses of speed reading. There are times when getting the detail is vital, and speed reading is not the right technique for those occasions. The same would also apply to reading for pleasure, or literary reading. There's a time and a place for everything, and speed reading and poetry are not compatible bedfellows.

Sense groups

Look at this passage below to get the feel of taking in more that a single word at a time. You can easily train your eye to jump from sense group to sense group quickly.

When talking/whether formally or informally / to a group / of people/ it is essential / to move your gaze / so that each / receives some / eye contact and /therefore, feels included / in your presentation. Notice how /professional entertainers / regularly take in /the entire audience / from stalls to gallery / in order to ensure that / nobody feels excluded.

The inability to provide / eye contact with an audience/ is one of / the major drawbacks / of reading from a script. Working from cards / or brief notes / is a far more effective / method of delivery.

Bulletin Board

Everyone can train themselves to read faster. The

techniques are simple, all that is required is the motivation to do them for a short time every day. Indeed, most people can practice as they read their daily mounds of incoming mail. Without even increasing reading speed it is possible to dramatically reduce the amount of time you spend digesting written material by being very selective in your choice, and reviewing systematically before diving into the detail.

Don't spoil a good piece of literature though, by hurrying yourself – but even here your trained 'slower' reading speed will be much quicker than those who have not bothered to save themselves valuable hours every week by adopting these simple techniques. Just think, saving only 15 minutes a day will give you the equivalent of a 40 hour working week in a year!

All glory comes from daring to begin

Business sense

All of the key commentators agree that the successful organisations of the new millennium have to be quick on their feet, nimble and flexible. But at the very same time many are struggling to manage the overwhelming volume of information and data coming into them from the ever-growing channels of communication.

Information, wanted or not, is coming at us from all sides. Sorting the 'wheat from the chaff' has never been more important. But how to do it? Companies are increasingly recognising the importance of 'knowledge management' the discipline of organising and utilising intellectual assets to create value.

In a recent survey of more than 400 senior American and European executives 87% said they were working in knowledge intensive businesses, but 96% believed that they could get much more out of the knowledge already inside their organisation if they learned how to use it creatively. The 'hard nosed' financial markets agree.

A recent analysis of leading Fortune 500 companies shows that most of their market value is now based, not on their capital equipment or physical assets, but on their *intellectual capital*. What that term covers is the info they hold in their databases or processes, their customers' knowledge and opinions of them – and last, but by no means least, the stuff their people are carrying around in their heads.

The most sophisticated organisations are now full steam ahead in implementing 'knowledge management' systems which try to make sense of what's coming into and going out of their organisation. It's not easy. What is irrelevant to one colleague is a nugget of vital information to another, and so it goes.

We can't rely on full time 'knowledge managers' (yes, there are such people, and the population is growing like topsy) to tell us what's useful. Only we can decide.

What is clear, however, is that the employee who digests information slowly is handicapping him or herself just as surely as if they donned a deep-sea diver's boots for a hundred metre dash. Like the 'top dog' athletes we need speed and agility. Speed reading is not just a gimmick, it's a must.

Training in the discipline could save organisations millions in wasted time – time that could be liberated for practical, action-oriented use. The champion's option is not to ignore communication because you feel swamped; there is no quality control in that approach (but many adopt it). Rather, the route to the winning line in this case is to hone your skills to the extent that you can flash read everything you feel is relevant, and still have time to spare. Why not throw the lead boots away?

The five 'killer' questions

Am I . . . .?	Yes	No	Maybe
Reading fast enough to really cope with the demands on me?			
Using the techniques that have produced speeds of 600 words a minute?			

Seeing the real personal and business benefits in absorbing information faster?			
Practising every day with my existing reading material?			
Going to go on a course to really get the skills under my belt?			
What am I going to do next?			

Why wouldn't you want to read faster at work and free yourself from the shackles of absorbing information. We all have to do it to a greater or lesser degree, so think of what you would do with the time created by your 'lightening fast' reading, and make doing that thing your reward.

Chapter 6

Develop a mega memory

In this chapter . . .

- **Learn how to use your memory to the full**
- **Discover how you think in 'ridiculous pictures'**
- **Beef up your ability to remember facts, figures and people**
- **Have fun remembering fifteen objects in sequence – forwards or backwards – after seeing them only once**

This is an age that discourages us from using our memory and thinking for ourselves. Our jobs are being replaced by computers, we use calculators, pocket organisers and other electronic wizardry to get the information we need, and all the time we keep our own computer – the most powerful of all – our brain, in its box hardly used.

> ***"A man's real possession is his memory. In nothing else is he rich, in nothing else is he poor"***
> Alexander Smith

The paradox is that the faster and more complex the world becomes, the more we need to use our brain to regain control over our lives.

Competition for jobs and business has probably never been fiercer. Your memory can help you to stand out from the crowd, to interact successfully with people, and to manage your life more effectively. A powerful memory is our brain's gift to us, if we choose to use it.

Have you ever felt a fool because you've forgotten the name of the business contact you were introduced to only seconds before? Ever got annoyed because you couldn't remember the telephone number of a key contact and you've forgotten your little black book? Ever had a great idea, not written it down and promptly forgotten it . . . .of course you have!

The vast majority of us have an average memory and are using at most 10% of its capacity. Studies by psychologist Mark Rosenweig concluded that if we fed in ten new items of information *every second* for a lifetime, the average brain would be only half full. Memory problems, he says, are not caused by the capacity of our brain but our management of the remembering process.

The truth is that our memory has become lazy and, unless we have developed memory techniques which help us to use it properly we are nowhere near as good as we could be. Without a trained memory we tend to keep information in our brains for the shortest possible time, and our memory is literally like a sieve.

Our lack of retention means that we are wasting valuable time constantly re-learning things we should already know. Tests prove that most of us forget 90% of the names of people we've just met, and at least 95% of phone numbers given to us.

> ***"I feel assured that there is no such thing as ultimate forgetting. Traces once impressed upon the memory are indestructible"***
> Thomas De Quincey

The irony is that we often forget those very things we need to retain, and it appears that our memory is faulty. In fact we all have a nearly perfect memory. Everything we've ever experienced is stored somewhere in our brain, and experiments from hypnotic regression to surgical stimulation of specific parts of the brain have proved this.

The problem is not our memory, it's our *recall*, and we simply can't recall the bulk of the information our memory has stored away for us. Why?

Try this: if a beautiful woman dressed only in a green thong came up to you on a packed commuter train, kissed you full on the lips for 10 seconds and slapped you in the face as hard as she could afterwards, do you think you would remember that for the rest of your life? Yes? Then why can't you remember the first sentence of this section (test yourself!).

> ***"Our thoughts are so fleeting that no device for trapping them should be overlooked"***
> Henry Hazlitt

The problem is, as Henry Hazlitt put it, 'Our thoughts are so fleeting that no device for trapping them should be overlooked.'

He advocated giving your memory a metaphorical 'slap in the face' – can you visualise that . . . imagine yourself slapping your memory. Literally, to make it do something (like a jockey slaps a horse to make it run faster). If you can 'see' that picture you're using the technique that all memory experts use – it's called 'ridiculous association'. A ridiculous picture helps to create effective attention, and it is this that causes you to notice and retain the thing you want to remember.

Think again about what happened to you on the train a moment ago. Why did you remember? Things like that simply don't happen, it was a ridiculous scenario. It also had action in it, and feeling (kiss and pain . . . whatever else is up to your imagination!) It would have been an even stronger memory if the image you had of the woman was larger than life (8 feet tall with attributes to match) – or there were a hundred of them all lining up to do the same thing to you. Can you see it?

The secret to memory is using your gift of imagination and having the systems in place to make facts memorable. You do not have to learn things by rote any more, or read things three times until half of the information sinks in, only to be forgotten the next week. You can retain it all by using your imagination to the full.

A good memory gives you the edge, it's impressive and practical and gets you noticed. Others in your organisation or business circles probably have had the same education and training as you, and are exposed to the same information on a daily basis. How then, can you get ahead? Using your memory better is one sure way. You don't need to be twice as good, just demonstrably better – knowledge is power, as the old saying goes.

With a little practice you can soon get to the stage of 'unconscious competence' where you use your memory automatically to remember your 'to do' lists without writing them down, names and other details of your business contacts, and any other piece of information you wish to retain and recall.

If you want to lick your memory into shape and have fun at the same time, here's how. As Harry Lorraine, the great memory expert and entertainer once said, ' New knowledge is acquired by being connected to something we already know. New things are remembered by being associated with something we already know.'

And the best way to associate the thing you want to remember with something you already know is to use pictures with as many of the following elements as you can. Let's be ridiculous!

- **Exaggerate it** – make the item huge, out of proportion, horrible, ear-splittingly loud, etc.
- **Put action in to the picture** – get the object moving, crashing, spinning, sticking, etc. . . . see it in your mind's eye.
- **Use all of your senses** – see it, smell it, taste it, feel it, hear it.
- **Make it brighter** – vivid colour is massively more memorable than dull and boring.
- **Add humour** – the sillier, more absurd and ridiculous the image, the easier it will be to recall.
- **Mix in sex and vulgarity** – anything which turns you on, or repulses you, will be very easily remembered.
- **Put things on top** – or underneath or inside one another, or substitute one thing for another.
- **Keep it simple** – don't add too many irrelevant images or they'll confuse your recall.

"The true art of memory is the art of attention"
Samuel Johnson

Jonathan Hancock, the Guinness Book of Records 1994 memory champ, says there are four golden rules of memory. You remember:

1. Things that happen to you
2. Things you can see
3. Unusual things
4. Things that fit into patterns

Here's a practical example; be prepared to let your imagination go, and you'll be amazed at the power of your memory. Normally you would be very unlikely to be able to remember 15 unassociated items in sequence after seeing them only once. If you could manage this feat, you would be even more unlikely to be able to retain them for any length of time afterwards. But after this exercise that's exactly what you will do, using the techniques highlighted above. We'll be creating ridiculous mental pictures that will allow you to easily recall the following items in order:

1. **table**
2. **book**
3. **bottle**
4. **chair**
5. **fish**
6. **telephone**
7. **window**
8. **sock**
9. **computer**
10. **radio**
11. **dish**
12. **pie**
13. **tractor**
14. **teapot**
15. **carpet**

Let's have some fun . . .

To remember the items in sequence we need to have a method of linking them together, rather like a daisy chain. In this way picturing one item reminds you of the next, and so on.

Picture the first item (table) in your mind's eye: really 'see' it. What kind of table is it: new old, wood or other material, big, small? Really 'see' it.

Now we need to link the new information to what we already know (table), as that is the whole principle of memory. We want to remember 'book', so we must form an association in our mind between **table and book**. Make your link as ridiculous and outrageous as possible. You may 'see' your table as one gigantic book, or a table made of millions of tiny books with pages constantly turning and knocking your dinner into your lap. Or picture yourself reading a gigantic table instead of a book – it's so heavy your arms are hurting!

Choose one image that appeals to you and form that association between table and book by seeing the picture in your mind's eye. Laugh out loud if you want . . . you've now linked table with book.

Let's do the same by linking **book to bottle**. See yourself pouring thousands of books instead of wine out of a bottle, or a book staggering along the road drunk, with a dozen bottles in each arm, smashing them as it lurches along. Hear the bottles crash to the ground. Please, be as bizarre as you like, but really 'see' the picture vividly in your mind, that's the secret. Logical images don't work because they are not memorable enough.

Link **bottle with chair** by seeing yourself relaxing in your lounge on a chair made out of beer bottles, smell the stale ale, feel the drips down your neck and the wet carpet under your feet. Or see a wine waiter in a restaurant pouring your wine from one of the legs of a chair and asking if you would like to taste it before serving!

Associate **chair to fish**. See a gigantic fish sitting on your chair, and there's no way he will move – or picture yourself sitting on a large fish (smell the fish, feel its scales . . . it's still alive, of course).

To take stock, we're always linking the present object to the previous one, new knowledge to existing knowledge. So far we've linked table to book, to bottle, to chair, to fish. Review all the outrageous connections in your mind before we go further.

Now link **fish to telephone**. You're holding a fish to your ear instead of the telephone; you're dialling the number with a huge fish instead of your finger or, when you answer the telephone millions of rotting fish fly out of the handset at you – feel them hitting your face, smell them, taste them!

Telephone to window. You can't see out of your house because huge telephones have attached themselves to each window pane and all are ringing at the same time (incongruity and a sense of the totally impossible are the foundation of remembering).

Window to sock. You're putting on socks with panes of glass in them. You have to close the windows in your socks to get them on properly, but they break, cutting your feet when you attempt to put your shoes on. See the blood, feel the pain.

Sock to computer. You go into the office to switch on your computer and millions of sweaty socks burst through the screen. Or your computer is now so small that you operate it from its location in the big toe of your sock, to the amazement of your friends. See yourself pressing the keys.

Computer to radio. Instead of music coming out of your radio when you switch it on you get millions of tiny computers all dancing and singing on the airwaves.

Radio to dish. You're eating your breakfast out of a radio instead of a dish, pour the milk on, and hear the gurgling noise of the radio.

Dish to pie. See yourself eating a pie, but as you bite into it, it turns into a porcelain dish and breaks your teeth. Hear the crack, feel it in your mouth, spit it out . . . ugh!

Pie to tractor. Picture a pie driving a tractor instead of a farmer. It waves to you and says good morning (smell it, what kind of pie is it, take a bite as it goes past).

Tractor to teapot. You're pouring tea out of a tractor's engine instead of a teapot, or a tea pot is ploughing a field, pouring cups of tea for cows as it goes past (the cows might even be holding their china cups out). The more ridiculous the image, the better.

Can you see it?

Teapot to carpet. Walk on hundreds of teapots in your home instead of the carpet. Hear the noise your shoes make. These teapots are slippy. Or see yourself pouring tea out of a rolled up carpet instead of a tea pot, spilling it on everyone as you go . . . it's so hot!

That's the 15 items linked together. Now, start at table and simply recall the link you made with the next item. Did you remember book? What does book remind you of? If your associations were strong enough you'll remember all of them, not just now, or tomorrow, but next week or even next year. A quick glance at the word to review the connections will bring back all the ridiculous associations you made. You could even do the list backwards now if you wanted. Give it a try!

Bulletin Board

The 15 items above are everyday objects, but this little exercise demonstrates the latent power of your memory with very little training. Your memory is possibly your most under utilised asset, and one of the easiest skills to develop quickly. Make the most of it if you want to get ahead quickly. All it needs is a little training and practice.

Look at the books listed in the Further Reading section and resolve to devote just a few minutes a day to building your memory 'muscle'. There couldn't be a more enjoyable way to significantly improve your performance.

Business sense

Every salesperson knows that they have lost a potential sale at one time or another through forgetting a contact's name or some key item of relevant information. Kicking oneself after the event may help relieve the feelings of frustration but it won't get the lost sale back, It's gone forever.

Also gone forever is anything that we do not make a strong enough association with in our mind. And the problem for many organisations and their employees is not just the vitally important social (and business-winning) aspects of remembering names, faces and company information, it is the time taken re-visiting information that could (should?) have been committed to memory . . . telephone numbers, key contacts and their positions, sales and financial figures, the location of reports – electronic or hard copy, you know the score.

Mundane? Maybe. But consider the moral of this story told by Harry Lorrayne about a rookie stockbroker going for a new job at a top city firm. The competition for the role was intense. No doubt past record, personality and potential were all being taken into account when the candidates were wheeled in.

But he got the job, hands down, no question. Why? Because he had memorised (easily, in half an hour) the names of the firm's major clients, its board members and their specialisms and key facts about the firm and its vision of the future – facts that were available to anyone.

But he amazed the panel with his knowledge (he knew more than some of them) and came across as a hugely intelligent, highly motivated and committed individual whose talents would be a great asset to their business. All for half an hour's (enjoyable) mental exercise.

Your memory, and those of the rest of your team, could be your greatest sales, efficiency and influencing asset. Are you taking the time to use it – or are you still looking for that missing report!

Before you go, why not try to memorise all of the following in order? It's the same technique as before. Be crazy (because crazy works)

1. Dog
2. Cup
3. Door
4. Motorcycle

5. Umbrella
6. Fork
7. Grandma
8. Priest
9. Tyre
10. Mini skirt
11. Crocodile
12. President Clinton
13. Baby
14. Cricket bat
15. Washing powder
16. Cork
17. Apple
18. Santa's grotto
19. Mouse
20. Your boss (if you have one, if not use God!)

All we're doing here is exercising your memory muscle and proving to you that you can, indeed, perform (relatively easily) feats you probably thought were impossible. Just think how good you could be with a bit of focused practice!

The five 'killer' questions

Am I . . . ?	Yes	No	Maybe
Using my memory capacity to the full?			
Consciously choosing to remember things using 'crazy' connections?			
Setting a short time aside every day to strengthen my memory using these techniques?			
Using 'props' like diaries and 'to do' lists less?			

Going to go on a course to really get the skills under my belt?			
What am I going to do next?			

Anyone can strengthen their memory. All that's required is a focus on the task, the willingness to take a bit of a risk of forgetting, and the commitment of just a few minutes a day to practice. You don't need long – and your colleagues and friends will marvel at the results. With a bit of training you can remember a pack of cards in order after seeing them only once. Not very practical, but it's a fun way to strengthen your memory . . . and it goes down great at parties!

Chapter 7

Accelerate your learning ability

In this chapter . . .

- **Discover the secrets of total recall and retention**
- **Soak up information like a sponge**
- **Learn how to review notes so that the information sticks for as long as you want**
- **Operate at peak efficiency by knowing how your brain functions**

Whilst it is important in business to be able to remember the faces, names, facts and figures critical to our area of work, if we are studying we have a slightly different problem because memory is not the same as understanding.

> ***"No problem can stand the assault of sustained thinking"***
> Voltaire

We can read a book and completely understand it, but the next day we can recall only half of it, and a week later only the key points. A month later we may not even remember reading the material in the first place!

Studies have proved that our recall gets worse over time. Cast your mind back to when you last studied for exams. You probably wasted an enormous amount of time and effort reading and understanding texts and notes only to forget the information shortly after the exam.

"The way you manage information will ultimately determine your competitiveness in the new Millennium"
Shaun Orpen
Marketing Director,
Microsoft

You can keep your recall at a peak if you know how. Using the right technique will save you hours, days or even months of study time – time that you can then devote to other areas of your life. It will also give you the edge in your work and ensure that you can remember at will what you have learned – the vast majority of your colleagues can't.

All of the advice below is based on scientific research into memory and recall, the key points of which are:

- We recall more at the start and end of learning periods; more of items which we can already associate with, and more of the things which are unusual or out of the ordinary (we proved this, of course, in the previous section).
- We recall very much less of the things in the middle of learning

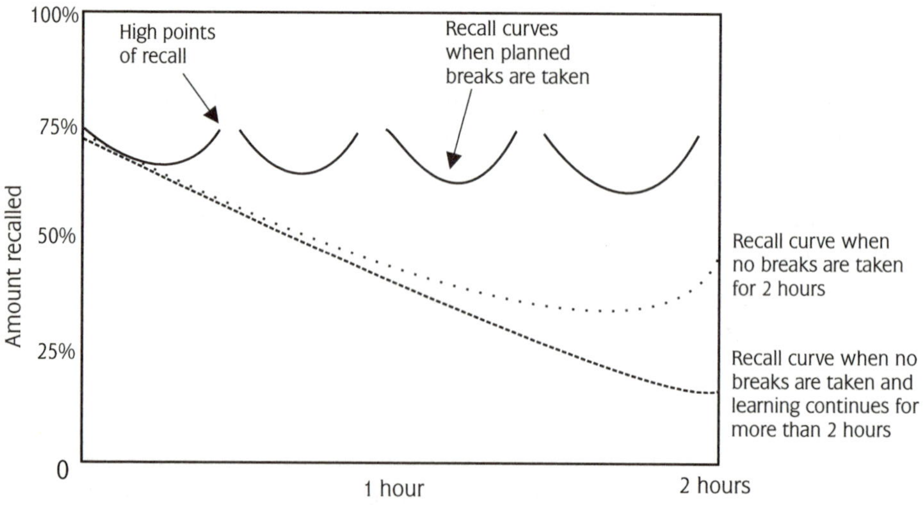

Figure 7.1

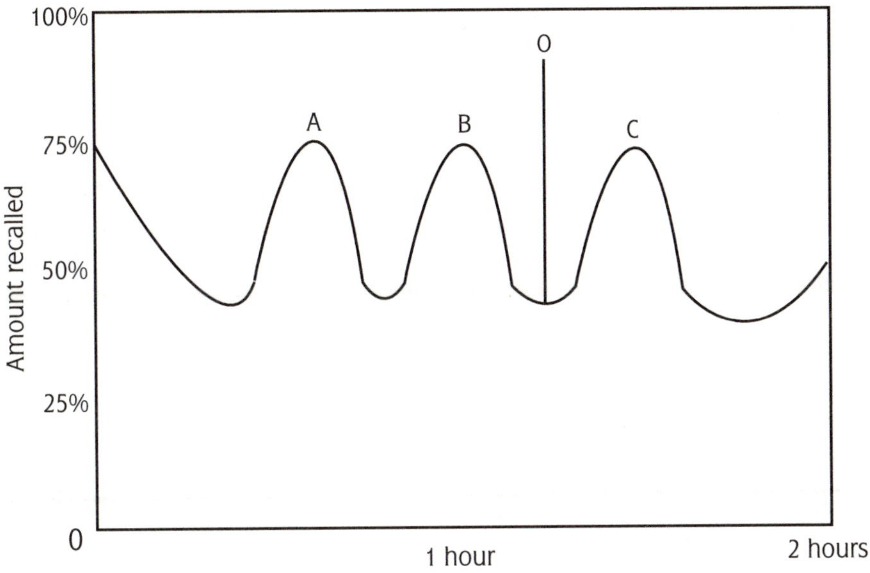

Figure 7.2 A, B and C are associated items linked by previous knowledge; O is an 'out of the ordinary' fact or piece of information.

periods, and those things that are mundane, dull and 'run of the mill'.

- The learning time that suits our brain best is between 20 and 40 minutes. This fact is critical for organisers of training and seminars, and is a vital platform for anyone studying to retain knowledge. (Look at Figure 7.1.)
- A small break of 5–10 minutes is enough to rest and refresh the brain and help it to retain the information we have learned.
- Recall after a learning period rises shortly afterwards, but then goes into free fall very quickly, with as little as 20% of the information being retained after only one day – what a waste of time and effort! (See Figure 7.2.)

The great news is that these studies have also encouraged the development of techniques for maintaining the level of recall at the highest possible level – between 75 and 90 % depending on the type of information to be recalled. The secret is to *review*.

To keep your recall at its optimum you need to review the material you have studied on a systematic basis. Do your first review 10 minutes after your initial learning session. This review should last 10 minutes, and will serve to keep your memory topped up for a day.

Next day review the material for 5 minutes, and this should keep you at peak recall for a week. Do another 5 minutes at the end of the week and you'll have the information locked in for a month. A month later take another 5 minutes, by that time the information should be well ingrained in you long term memory. Review after that only when you feel the need.

But how do you review, you might ask? Your first review should be a thorough and complete note revision, making amends and comments as you go. Your other reviews will take a different form – and this is where you will see the value of revision like this. For your second and later reviews, take a piece of paper and, without referring to your original notes, write down everything you can recall.

Do it in mind map form, it's much easier and massively aids retention. Taking notes in the normal way only uses your 'logical' left brain, and the sentences, paragraphs and lines tend to make the material unmemorable. Mind maps, on the other hand, make use of your 'creative' right brain as well and bring it to life with originality, colour and association . . . all the things your memory loves as 'hooks' to help it recall.

Failure to prepare is preparation for failure

Compare your review with your original notes. The simple act of trying to recall, and doing something practical, makes a huge difference to your retention. Reviewing in this way means that you'll feel in control of your material, gain immense confidence from the knowledge you have already retained, and will be in a much stronger position to build on the things you already know.

Anything that you do have difficulty recalling can be worked on using the memory techniques outlined earlier. Reviewing like this is easy and efficient, and it will help you to make great strides in building your knowledge base quickly. Remember, the more you know, the easier it is to absorb and associate new information – it's a virtuous circle well worth cultivating.

Bulletin Board

Accelerated learning has more to do with technique than natural ability. Using these scientifically proven ways of working you will significantly boost your potential to retain and recall information.

Review properly and systematically and the information will be stored in your long-term memory for as long as you desire. There is no need to ever again be in the position where all you have learned has 'disappeared' from your memory.

Business sense

Most business people never go back and re-read what they have already read, unless the material is critical to them or is used as a key element of their role – legislation for lawyers, etc. But as we've seen, and the scientists have proven, for the little you recall (without systematic review) it's almost not worth reading the stuff in the first place.

There is no shortcut. Victory lies in overcoming obstacles every day

The conundrum is that we all need to keep up with the plethora of news, information, statistics and facts that enable us to do our job. The problem in the way we go about it is that hoping to remember key pieces of information without a systematic approach is like trying to retain water in a leaking bucket . . . it simply won't work.

With competition for jobs so fierce these days – the massive redundancies are still going on as global and big national organisations merge and downsize – there is no room for complacency anywhere; and that includes the boardroom.

Leaders want people who know what they are talking about, people with command of their facts, competent people who know about the business. What better and easier way to ensure that you are in this position than using these techniques?

They work, the scientists have proved that they are easier to apply than any other method you learned at school. Why not take the time to make review part of your routine? The discipline may, or may not, help you to keep your present job – but there's no doubt that it will give you a grounding in mental ability that will put you head and shoulders above your colleagues in your business or sector that are still adopting the leaking bucket approach.

The five 'killer' questions

Am I . . . ?	Yes	No	Maybe
Really convinced that this accelerated learning stuff will work?			
Intent on using it as part of my daily routine?			
Identifying the things I really must retain, and using the techniques?			
Applying the principles of attention span to the way I conduct meetings?			
Telling my people about them so that we can all benefit?			
What am I going to do next?			

The scientists have proved that this stuff works, so it's not just someone's opinion on how to do it. Why not have a go by doing a quick review of the key points of this chapter and prove to yourself that the information really does 'stick'. Help your memory to help you.

Where am I now?

Success Secret No. 2, release your potential, means rediscovering your natural creativity and the ability to soak up information like a sponge. We had it when we were kids. We can have it again. All it takes is confidence, the willingness to look foolish if we are wrong, and to have 'good tries'.

The psychologists have proved that we learn best and retain more by using the techniques covered here. But being creative is only the second piece of the 'success' jigsaw. Now we need to learn how to use our new found creativity constructively . . . by making things happen.

Barefoot on broken glass

Creative use of my imagination was a critical element in developing my ability to walk barefoot on broken glass.

I visualise myself walking effortlessly across the glass, I 'see' myself liking the experience and recall all the other times I have successfully achieved the feat. Most importantly, I 'see' the glass and 'feel' it as if it were 12ft of crushed ice . . . sharp, but with a numbing effect. It works!

We can achieve so much with creativity, and can achieve nothing without it. Check out the website **www.barefootbook.com** *for more ways to enhance your creativity.*

Secret 3

Make things happen

"Perhaps the most valuable result of all education is the ability to make yourself do the thing you have to do when it ought to be done – whether you like it or not.

It is the first lesson that ought to be learned and however early a person's training begins, it is probably the last lesson a person learns thoroughly"

Thomas Huxley

Chapter 8

Set and achieve big goals

In this chapter . . .

- **How to get to where you want to be by setting goals**
- **Uncover the four reasons why you may have never set goals before**
- **Learn techniques to get you moving and keep you on track**

The Yale University research highlighted earlier (p. 18) gave undisputed evidence that the 3% of the population who set goals for themselves achieved many times more than those who didn't. It seems then that the discipline of goal setting is the critical difference between major success and the mere average. Those who set goals and wrote them down kept them at the forefront of their mind and central to their lives. They kept their passion and their daily work and thoughts were guided in the direction they wished to go.

> *"If one advances confidently in the direction of their dreams, and endeavours to lead a life which they have imagined, they will meet with a success unexpected in common hours"*
> Henry David Thoreau

Very few people have a real passion that drives them on day after day. We tend to suffer from the negative influence of the world around us, the people close to us, and our own comfort zone. Many of us find that goal setting is an uncomfortable and unnatural process; we haven't been taught the techniques and are unsure what we want, or how to go about realising our aspirations.

We need the help of tools that allow us to discover our goals and focus our energies upon them.

Setting and achieving goals to create a 'step change' in your life will be the aim for some readers. For others, however, 'making things happen' will be about creating incremental gains in just one area of your life or business. It doesn't matter which route you take, the goal setting technique is the same. It all boils down to identifying what you really want for yourself. You've got to be comfortable with, and motivated by, your goals because without these factors you won't be able to generate the passion and commitment needed to get the results you desire.

> ***"My principal motive has been to get into a venture because I enjoy the challenge of doing it better than others"***
> Richard Branson

Sadly, many people concentrate what goal setting they do undertake on the wrong areas. For instance, people generally spend more time planning their wedding than they do the marriage, and more time deciding where to go on holiday than on planning what to do with the rest of their lives.

There are four big reasons why 97% of folk don't have clear goals.

1. **Fear.** They reckon that it is no use setting goals because nothing good is going to happen to them anyway.
2. **They have a poor image of themselves**. They can't imagine that they could do the things they want to do; their self-image simply won't let the 'see' the possibilities.
3. **They have never been encouraged to see the value** – no one ever told them that goal setting really works.

4. **They don't know how to do it** – but as we'll see here the process really is simple; we can all set goals in any area of our life.

"Would you tell me please which way I ought to go from here?" "That depends a good deal on where you want to get to" said the cat. "I don't much care . . ." said Alice "Then it doesn't matter which way you go" said the cat.
From *Alice in Wonderland* by Lewis Carroll

The 3% who had decided what they wanted for themselves followed five practical steps. They:

1. Wrote down their goals.
2. Listed the obstacles they needed to overcome.
3. Identified the people and organisations who could help them get there.
4. Created a plan of action.
5. Put dates on when they would achieve actions on the way; and regularly monitored their plan.

US Senator George J. Mitchell, Chairman of the peace talks in Northern Ireland, brought all of this goal setting to poignant life. After two years of the most intense and frustrating discussion and debate between proud leaders in the Province, the Good Friday peace plan was finally signed.

"Always bear in mind that your resolution to success is more important than any other thing"
Abraham Lincoln

'The Good Friday agreement was the realisation of a dream for me', said the Senator.

> 'Now it's a reality I have a new dream . . . one day I will go with my young son to Ireland; I will sit in the Parliament building and watch, and listen, as the politicians debate the ordinary issues of the day. No talk of war. No talk of peace. There will be no need. Peace will be taken for granted.'

A powerful vision from the man voted the most respected member of the Senate for six consecutive years, a crystal clear and liveable goal.

"Far better to dare mighty things, to win glorious triumphs even though chequered by failure, than to rank with those poor spirits who neither enjoy nor suffer much because they live in the grey twilight that means neither victory nor defeat"
Theodore Roosevelt

Now back to you. Try these questions to get your goal setting juices flowing:

- If you could do anything what would it be?
- If you could be anyone, who would you be?
- What would you do if you knew you couldn't fail?
- What will your life be like five or ten years from now? (What will you have achieved, what relationships will you have, how will you have got there?)

You will be *somewhere* in five years; do you know where you want to be? Are you going to trust to luck, or guide your direction of travel by writing down your heart's desire?

As Zig Ziglar, one of the great goal-setting speakers says, 'You can't make it as a "wandering generality" you have to become a meaningful specific.'

"How you organise your future has an awful lot to do with your future"
Watts Wacker, futurist

Try some of these headings to give you a feel for the areas in which you may want to set goals. They help to get you down to the specifics of what you want out of life.

Key goal-setting areas

- **Career**
  What kind of job, where, earning how much, with what benefits?
- **Family**
  Strength of relationship, children, shared time, holidays . . . fun!
- **Home**
  Where, style, size, cost? See specifically what it will look like and what it will contain. Focus on the detail.
- **Friends and 'giving back'**
  Who, how you will support others, community work, lifestyle?

- **Personal wellbeing**
  Health, appearance, weight, habits, exercise, relaxation
- **Material matters**
  Money, car, savings, insurances and other trappings associated with success
- **Personal stuff**
  Self esteem and confidence, learning new skills or new things, religion, peace of mind, etc.

Turning your dreams into a series of small tasks, the 'salami' technique as it's known (imagine chopping a salami into fine slices) and putting deadlines on them, takes the 'wish' element out of goals and fills them with action power. Focusing on doing each small element takes you closer to your vision, helps you manage your comfort zone and reduces the inevitable feeling of 'I'll never get there.'

Using this approach and continuing to capture your goals on paper gives you the control and insight to measure your progress and revise, reschedule or even remove goals if they are no longer something you want to do. But remember also that when obstacles arise you should change the direction to reach the goal, not your decision to get there.

> ***"I am looking for a lot of men who have an infinite capacity to not know what can't be done"***
> Henry Ford

Writing down even small goals breathes life and reality into them. Achieving things doesn't happen without some effort, you need vision and inspiration coupled with tenacity and persistence. These are attributes your mind tends to move you away from and back toward comfort.

Many of us fail to take the action we need to take to move us closer to our goals simply because we tell ourselves we are 'not in the mood'.

There are two schools of thought on how to get tasks done. One is to take the hardest or most important first and to really concentrate all our energies on it; the other is to take an easy task first to 'break ourselves in' and get motivated. The choice is yours, but either is better than doing nothing!

Newton's law of momentum applies here (to paraphrase): 'Things at rest tend to remain at rest, things in motion tend to remain in motion.'

"Tentative efforts lead to tentative outcomes. Give yourself fully to your endeavours. "Decide to construct your character through excellent actions and determine to pay the price of a worthy goal. "Remain steadfast . . . and one day you will build something worthy of your potential"
Epictetus
Roman philosopher
AD 33–135

If you can't get yourself moving ask yourself why you are not doing it, and what you are going to do to get started. These are incisive questions which may throw up mental barriers to completing the task or moving closer to the goal – fear of failure, or ridicule, confrontation, disclosure, fear of risk . . . even fear of success! Whatever the reason, the only way forward is to have a go, and stretch that comfort zone as far as you can.

One example of a mental barrier to achieving goals is the running of the four-minute mile which was eventually cracked by Roger Bannister. For years the cream of the world's milers had struggled with this psychological barrier; many said it just couldn't be done, the human body couldn't stand it – but once Roger had done it there were several runners over the next couple of years who could claim the same feat. In fact running a sub-four-minute mile is now so commonplace that the New Zealander John Walker has recorded more than 100 himself!

The same process happened when pilot Chuck Yeager broke the sound barrier. Before he did it many sceptics predicted it was impossible and that Yeager and his Bell Aviation X-1 plane would end up in a thousand pieces. The reality is that the sound 'barrier' was a myth. And, as Yeager wrote, 'the real barrier wasn't in the sky, but in our knowledge of supersonic flight'.

Usually it is not a lack of time that's the problem in achieving goals, it is a lack of clear direction. When you have direction (and your goal setting exercise will give you this) it creates time – and motivation follows action, not the other way round. So don't wait until you feel like doing something, just do it and you'll soon feel charged up.

Bulletin Board

You can't underestimate the power of goals. They provide direction and focus to your life and your day to day actions. Write them down though – and review them often; that's the only way your brain will be convinced that you are really seriously committed to them. The Yale University research showed scientifically that goal setting does work. Make it work for you too.

The key is to avoid falling into the trap of being be a 'thinker/contemplator'. Be a doer instead. Take some action *now* to begin to achieve one of your goals, and make a point of enjoying it on the way. Don't live for anticipated fulfilment of your dreams, enjoy the ride too. And, of course, when you've reached a goal get on with setting another!

> *"We worked furiously to realise our goals. Because we didn't have fear we could do something dramatic"*
> Masaru Ibuka
> Sony Corporation founder

Business sense

Most people working in, or for, organisations have the capability to achieve massively more than their present role allows or requires. The way we manage people, on the whole, keeps them 'boxed in'. The organisations that are succeeding are those that have found the knack of releasing that latent potential, to trust their people, to motivate them and help them to really contribute to the corporate dream.

Picture a casino in Las Vegas, where hundreds of gamblers stand at slot machines. Each is interested in only the machine he (she) is playing. Why? Because he has a stake in that machine. An organisation's employees are just the same. The bigger their stake in the business, the more they will stretch to capture the rewards.

Unfortunately, all to often, incentive plans that could motivate only serve to frustrate and confuse. They lose sight of the real objective, to energise and focus behaviour.

By aligning workforce incentives with his organisation's real priorities VTEL's CEO, Dick Moeller, forged an early concentration on creating value for shareholders in the merger with Compression Labs. Early communication of these incentives to his people boosted the focus, enthusiasm and support of workers on both sides of the deal.

> ***"Everybody in an organisation needs to feel like they are an owner. Trust, and success, comes from people taking responsibility"***
> Harpal Randhawa
> Antfactory, E-Business and venture capital provider

Another great example of what can be achieved by getting your people involved is Transco. The birth of Transco may have produced the biggest 'start up' in the history of business. With assets of £17bn Transco, when it was created, shot into the top 30 biggest companies in the UK. Formed by the dismantling of 12 regional gas entities and moving from public sector status, it has boosted productivity per employee by 15% in each of the last three years, whilst reducing operating costs by 9% a year.

It has come smiling through tremendous cultural and organisational change. So what's the secret?

> ***"Companies need to have a strategic intent – to have an aspiration that is widely shared, to have a goal which is clear and to have an obsession with winning – that is the fuel that drives the engine"***
> C. K. Pralahad

'I think it was because we tried to involve everybody in what we were doing', says MD Harry Moulson, who has grown up in the gas business. 'You've got to have a goal, and it's absolutely vital that you have a mission which you are trying to achieve. You have to really communicate what the goal and mission actually are.'

It seems then that the secret of corporate success is identical to that of personal success – to set a goal, create a big dream (a vision) and keep the direction constantly in mind.

Sony knows the score on this point. Talking about the factors that keep Sony at the top of a hugely competitive worldwide electronics market, head of R&D Dr Makato Kikuchi tells it like this.

> 'The difference between our efforts and those of other companies lies not in the level of technology, or the quality of our people, or even the amount budgeted [for R&D]. The main difference lies in the establishment of mission-oriented research and proper *targets*. Many other companies give their researchers full freedom. We don't. We find an aim, a very real and clear target, and then establish the necessary task forces to get the job done. Ibuka [Sony's founder] taught us that – once commitment to go ahead is made, never give up. This pervades all R&D at Sony.'

Former chairman and CEO of Burger King, Barry Gibbons, knew the business value of setting goals, and measuring them. He and his team gave McDonald's a major shock simply by applying the credo 'what gets measured gets done . . . and what gets paid for gets done even more'.

That was the way that Gibbons got his people really focussed on service quality – that's what they were measured on, and paid for. His view? 'Raise awareness by the only method that is effective – build personal quality goals into personal objectives. If corporate quality goals were not met, no bonus of any kind got paid to anybody. Period.'

Tough but fair; crystal clear and focussed . . . and it worked.

> ***"Of all the things I have done, the most vital is co-ordinating the talents of those who work for us and pointing them towards a certain goal"***
> Walt Disney

The five 'killer' questions

Am I . . . ?	Yes	No	Maybe
Clear about how goal setting works?			
Writing mine down and reviewing them very frequently?			
Spending time visualising the outcome I want?			

Identifying the obstacles in the way of achieving my goals and addressing them?			
Breaking them into 'do-able' chunks so that I can see progress?			
What am I going to do next?			

"The message at Monsanto is clear . . . senior executives will not be rewarded unless the shareholders win. We have granted traditional stock options to all our employees, not just our senior managers"

The **www.barefootbook.com** website is the place to go for more info on the 'how to's' of goal setting. It needn't take long to clarify what you want and, just as important, what you *don't* want to achieve. Once you've got that clear sense of direction you can start to visualise the outcome in your mind's eye and take the 'do-able' steps needed to get you there. But how do you motivate yourself to do something. Let's have a look . . .

Chapter 9

Strengthen your 'do it' muscle

In this chapter . . .

- **How to strengthen your inner resolve**
- **Practical ways to exercise your 'do it' muscle every day**
- **Alter your mindset and increase your energy and vitality**

Everything in life revolves around only two issues; to choose to do something or to choose not to.

The problem with reading books about 'how to do it' is that while you are reading, you are not actually doing the thing you are learning to do. For some of us reading about how it's done provides all the emotional comfort we need. We rationalise: 'I've got the knowledge now, I can do it, but now is not the right time (insert one of 100 plausible excuses) but I'll get round to it soon.' Our minds become happy with the thought that we don't need to exert ourselves, and the illusion of progress has been created!

> ***Do or not do***
> ***There is no try"***
> Yoda

We live in an increasingly hedonistic society where, for many, our purpose appears to be to avoid struggle and strain and gain immediate gratification of our desires with little or no effort.

We're driven by comfort. Central heating, air conditioning, car washes, computers, TV, calculators (you name it) are all designed to make our lives more comfortable.

We can control or even block out pain through drugs, or take 'recreational' drugs which purport to help us feel better about ourselves and our world. In short, we have developed many goods and services to help us avoid the effort of using our own resources.

Each of us has a reservoir of energy . . . the power to get things done, and achieve results. Use it and it will replenish itself. Avoid using it and it stagnates, making it increasingly difficult to draw off the energy we need to get the results we want.

Recognise though, that to do something you need inner resolve – willpower – and willpower is weakened as you gravitate towards comfort. We have to use self-discipline to strengthen our 'do it' muscle.

This means getting tough with ourselves and, sometimes, to do things we really don't want to do. Sadly, we've been conditioned to believe that if we don't feel like doing something it's OK. To achieve our goals we need to break free from the feeling, overcome our own inertia, and get on with the job.

> ***"You can't build a reputation on what you are going to do"***
> Henry Ford

Here's a good example of what happens when we're jolted out of our 'do nothing' mindset. Picture the scene:

You've just come home depressed and exhausted after a hard day at the office, had dinner on your lap and now you're loafing on the settee watching TV. The phone rings: it's your old friend who you haven't seen for months who is in town for one night only and insists on coming round to tell you the latest news. You put the phone down and spend a frenzied half-hour tidying the house and getting yourself ready. The door bell rings, and there to greet your friend is the smiling, energetic you – a different person to half an hour before.

By the close of a very late evening you've regained your energy and vitality and had a great time! You were forced out of your lethargy because you had to respond to the situation. And if you can do it when forced, the trick is to be able to do it yourself when the need arises, to help you to move towards your goals instead of giving in to the seductive lure of comfort, (which usually means avoiding what you know you really should be doing).

> ***"We act as though comfort and luxury were the chief requirements of life, when all we need to make us happy is something to be enthusiastic about"***
> Charles Kingsley

Sure, there must be a place for relaxation and recreation in our lives too, time for 'hanging out' and doing nothing much. It's great to watch TV and essential to have some 'recovery time' as the stress experts call it; but we must keep that 'do it' muscle strong too, by regularly choosing to do things we really don't feel like doing but are on the path to our goals.

As one commentator has said, 'The difference between an unsuccessful person and others is not a lack of strength, not a lack of knowledge, but rather a lack of will.' Or, to put it another way, people don't fail because they intend to fail, they fail because they fail to do what they intend to do.

> ***"Opportunity is missed by most people because it is dressed in overalls and looks like work"***
> Thomas Edison

The opportunity to strengthen our 'do it' muscle happens hundreds of times a day. Every second we are doing *something*

But is it the right thing? Or have we chosen to avoid what we need to do in favour of moving towards comfort (less fear, exertion, exposure etc)?

Amazing as it may seem, the law of 'do it' applies to the mechanical world as well. Aerospace engineers tell us that an aeroplane sat on the tarmac doing nothing wears out faster than an identical one worked hard in the air – the one on the ground rusts, the other doesn't. You won't be surprised to know then that the same applies to ships. A port-ridden ship collects barnacles and becomes unseaworthy far quicker than if it had sailed the high seas. You no doubt get the obvious parallel. Use your mental and

> ***"We can always do better; We can always go further; We can always find new possibilities – you have to keep going, and doing"***
> Henry Ford

physical faculties to push yourself if you want to keep yourself in peak condition; saving yourself for the future is simply helping you to gather mental or physical barnacles.

Some of the best advice in this area came from the American psychologist William James. He was talking about the times when we are actually doing the thing we should be doing:

> 'Periodically, whilst we are doing it, our mind (ego, conscience, the little voice in our head) will attempt to sabotage our efforts saying "have a break" . . . "stop now, you've done enough" . . . "it's too much pressure" . . . "let's get a drink and rest a while" anything, in fact, to stop us doing the job in hand. Recognise the voice, listen to it, but turn down the volume or ignore it. Obeying it constantly can ruin your resolve and leave your dreams in tatters.'

Bulletin Board

The comfort zone will play up at your weakest point, and this is the moment of truth when you either choose to do something or choose not to do it. The simple message is to make a conscious effort to choose the actions that lie along the path to your goals. Once started, you'll get the motivation to continue, then just keep on going so that your focus is taken away from anything your comfort zone can throw at you.

Business sense

Creating conditions where you commit to doing something, where there is no question of turning back, is a key weapon in the business leader's and management consultant's armoury. It's called the 'burning platform' approach: picture an oil rig out in the middle of the North Sea which catches fire and you have to use all of your physical and emotional strength to jump and survive – and you get the idea of the power of this technique. It's been used by leaders for years to release and focus the energies of their 'troops' and to conjure up extraordinary commitment to the task in hand.

Take Julius Caesar in 49 BC, then the military governor of Gaul, who signalled his intention to overthrow the Roman state by crossing the Rubicon River (hence the origin of the saying 'crossing the Rubicon) and entering territory forbidden to Caesar and his army. To fail would have meant certain death; but the commitment – signalled in advance – filled his army with the passion and energy to succeed . . . they had no choice! It was the same when the Romans (literally) burned their boats as they landed on the beaches of Britain. They knew there was no turning back: the only way to survive was to fight and win. They knew a few things about motivation, those Romans.

> ***"The secret of getting ahead is getting started. The secret of getting started is breaking your complex overwhelming tasks into small manageable ones, and then starting on the first one"***
> Mark Twain

Today the tactic is applied to business where, as never before, commitment means the difference between success and failure. It's not just the presence of the goal that creates progress, it is the level of commitment to the goal that's critical to its achievement. Boeing's commitment to build the 727 – 'We'll build this aeroplane even if it takes the resources of the entire company' – says it all about their determination to succeed, no matter what the cost. Boeing's engineers created the 727 largely because they were given no other choice. The story goes like this . . .

> ***"In challenging yourself you learn things all the time"***
> Richard Branson

In the early 1960's Boeing turned the demands of a potential customer, Eastern Airlines, into a clear, precise and almost impossible challenge. Boeing management told its engineers to construct a jet that could land on runway 4-22 at New York's La Guardia Airport. At only 4,860 ft long, the runway was much too short for any existing passenger jet of the time.

That's not all. To add a bit of interest for the engineers the jet also had to be able to fly non-stop from New York to Miami *and* be wide enough for seating passengers six abreast *and* have the capacity of 131 passengers *and*, of course, meet US aviation regulations on engineering quality.

The point is that it would have been easy for Boeing to give up somewhere along the line, but it couldn't because it had made a commitment to achieve its goal. History now tells us that the company produced the jet that became the 'workhorse' of modern aviation worldwide.

There's a whole raft of financial and other incentives used by the top-performing organisations to get their people to commit to their vision. Share options, profit-related pay, on-target bonuses and promises of rapid promotion are all designed to engineer commitment and transcend our natural tendency to stay within what we believe we could, or should, be expected to achieve.

A few years ago, professors Michael Hannan and John Freeman wrote a book with the catchy title *Organisational Ecology*. Not for light readers, the book looked at the life and death of industries and the companies within them to see if there was a pattern. Using the complex mathematical modelling techniques used in the biological sciences they concluded that 'selection processes only work on available diversity'. Translated into a language that you and me understand, they found that all success boils down to trying more things (this is where the diversity bit comes in).

"Organisations that support diversity attract and retain the most talented people, and keep pace with a changing marketplace. But management must show a strong commitment to its inclusion in corporate plans. Lack of commitment can alienate people, create lower efficiency, decreases in effectiveness and decline in performance"
Mohamed Zainurba

Put simply, they said that unless you *do* something, you don't know if it will work. But most businesses and the people within them get stuck in the thinking and planning mode and live less in the area of 'just doing it'. The message from the scientists is that unless we're landing new tries – creating 'available diversity' all the time, we won't have much stuff to select from when we need to adapt to the gathering momentum of change.

The five 'killer' questions

Am I . . . ?	Yes	No	Maybe
Putting off things I know should be done?			
Consciously choosing to do the 'right' things?			
Trying new things frequently enough?			
Occasionally 'forcing' myself to do what I don't want to do so that I can strengthen my willpower?			
Breaking my tasks down into manageable 'bite sized' pieces			
What am I going to do next?			

As an exercise in strenthening your 'do it' muscle, why not resolve to do a job around the house that you've been putting off for ages, or call an old friend or a relative who you know you should keep in contact with. The task needn't be big, but you'll feel much better. If you don't fancy those two, how about tidying the garage or loft, or weeding out all the old stuff in your filing system. Mundane, yes, but doing things like this is simply a way of building the habit of doing what needs to be done even if it doesn't fill us with excitement!

Chapter 10

Focus and achieve more in less time

In this chapter . . .

- Create peace of mind through focus
- How to cope with increasing demands on your time
- Learn to recognise the important things in your life
- Simple ways to maintain your vision and motivation

What you accomplish in your life is the result of what you achieve in a single day. Time is our greatest resource both at work and at home, and we need time to achieve what we want. Techniques for managing our time have been around for decades, and there are literally hundreds of good techniques and practices. Why then are so many of us stressed by the volume of tasks we need to do?

> ***"Nothing contributes so much to tranquillising the mind as a steady purpose – a point upon which the soul may fix its intellectual eye"***
> Mary Shelley

If time management alone was the answer it would have made the difference by now. Unfortunately it can be a rigid, unnatural process and, for all but the most committed, the intensity of time management is hard to maintain.

No wonder that people have a tendency to hark back to the 'good old days' when we had 'more time', time to do things, increased leisure time, quality time at home with the family and so on. The fact is that we didn't have more time then and we don't have less time now – there are still only 24 hours in the day.

Today we have much more choice about how we spend our time because we can do things faster than ever. We have simply created the illusion that we have less time. In reality we now have more devices for saving time than in the history of the world, but still can't seem to get enough of it; we have become 'time bankrupts'.

The problem is that the faster we do something the sooner we face our next issue, and for many of us this is the grist of our daily working routine; scrambling up a mountain of tasks and striving to get over the top to put them behind us. But as soon as we've conquered one mountain another looms before us and again we rush to scale it in a perpetual attempt move forward.

The performance demands on us all have increased over the last decade, and we are never going to get rid of these metaphorical mountains in our working lives. However we've been told that if we keep working harder, doing things better, smarter and faster we'll be able to do it all and have the control and peace we need. Disappointingly, the end result is often increased frustration and guilt rather than the control we desperately seek.

A solution needs to be found before our working population falls victim to executive burn out and mental and emotional fatigue. A fundamentally different attitude to mountains of work is needed if we are to survive and thrive in the corporate environment of the future. Carefully selecting the mountains we are going to climb, and simply enjoying the view of the others is the secret. So let's start at the bottom.

You have 24 hours to play with in the day. Roughly one-third of it is taken up by eating, sleeping and personal hygiene. The rest is yours to do what you want with it – and the question at the heart of it all is what do you *really* want to do with it. *Achieving* more doesn't necessarily translate into *doing* more. Doing the right things is more important than doing things right. It's the difference between effectiveness (doing the right things) and efficiency (doing things right).

Avoiding climbing unnecessary mountains, and focusing your efforts on those you choose to scale means being a 'time miser'. Ask yourself these questions:

- What am I doing that doesn't really have to be done?
- What am I doing that someone else could do?
- Am I doing the 'right' things at work and home?
- What can I (or others) do more efficiently?
- What am I doing that wastes other people's time?

Eliminating time wasting and moving your focus away from those activities that are not bringing you closer to your personal or corporate goals probably means giving up some mountaineering along the way in favour of more exciting and challenging ones for you personally.

You'll already be familiar with the time management techniques of planning your day the previous evening, listing your objectives and tasks, prioritising and allocating time to them. You'll also have heard about building in 'concentration blocks' to allow you to do, and plan actions to move you closer to your goals. And you'll know the sound advice about having only one project on your desk at any one time so that you can focus without distractions. The critical factor, as always, is to put it into practice.

These are all practical tools designed to avoid being caught up in urgent matters which take your eye off the real question – are you doing the right things with your life, and are you devoting enough time to the really important matters. This six-step weekly planning process is the key.

> ***"Do the truly important first"***
> Ray Croc
> McDonald's founder

Every week set aside some time (Sunday evening is good) to:

1. Review your vision to reconnect with what is most important to you before you decide how you spend your next week. As a guide:
   - What do you care about?
   - What kind of person do you want to be?
   - What contribution do you want to make?
   - What feelings do you want in your life (peace, happiness, confidence)?

'See' the vision of the life you want to create

2. Review the roles you have in life. These could include: partner, family, work, community or other areas; and consider what it is most important for you to achieve in the next week. It is not necessary to allocate time to each area – you need balance, but the last thing you want to feel is that you are running so fast to spend time in each of the areas of your life that you are simply touching the bases, and some of the really important things or people are not getting the attention they deserve.

> ***"Things that matter most must never be at the mercy of things that matter least"***
> Goethe

Don't forget also that you need time to recuperate and increase your own capacity to produce results. Allocate some time to your own development, recreation, reading, social interaction – whatever you personally need to ensure that your contribution is at its peak.

3. Ask yourself, for each of your roles 'What is the most important thing I can do in this role over the next seven days'? (You may not need to set a goal in each area.)
4. Develop your plan for the week, making sure that urgent things do not dominate the weekly activities and 'push out' the important ones.
5. Protect your priorities. Each day many 'alternative' actions will

present themselves. Some will be urgent and important and will need to be dealt with, others won't. The constant challenge is to protect the important things you said you would do.

6. Close the loop. Evaluate how you did with your goals and use the review as a platform for planning the next week. Be objective, the idea is to learn from what you have or haven't achieved and plan accordingly.

"Procrastinaation is the fear of success. People procrastinate because they are afraid of the success that they know will result if they move ahead now. Because success is heavy, and carries a responsibility with it, it is much easier to procrastinate and live with the 'someday I'll' philosophy"
Denis Waitley

It is usually not through a lack of skill that we don't do the things we should do. Rather it is a lack of focus on the task itself. The excuses we give ourselves range from 'I've not got the time' through to 'I'm too tired' or 'I'll get round to it when I feel more like doing it'. We even blame other people: 'It's your fault I can't . . .'

Some of the reasons may have a realistic ring of truth, but more likely it's because we consciously or subconsciously choose to do something else with our time. This is not a book which psychoanalyses why we would make such choices – it would be a lot thicker if it did – but let's agree that we are all prone to put off big, challenging or un-enjoyable tasks. We put off small jobs as well!

"The heights by great men reached and kept were not attained by sudden flight but they, while their companions slept, were toiling upward in the night"
Henry Longfellow

Ninety per cent of the population has a 'butterfly' approach to life, settling on something for a short while until we are distracted or bored, and then off to the next source of interest . . . and the dance continues on and on. We have to train ourselves to concentrate for longer and to strengthen our ability to direct our attention.

Meditation helps enormously (see p. 120), not just for relaxation, but as a tool to beef up your ability to focus. Just try this: Sit in total silence for 20 minutes and be aware of your breathing, think of nothing else. How long was it before your mind wandered? Often it will be only a matter of seconds until a thought pops into your head and your mind is off elsewhere.

Distractions like these happen to us hundreds of times a day, and it's little wonder we can't concentrate and finish a job we know we really should do. Thankfully a little self-awareness rolled up with some practical tips can make a world of difference to our productivity.

Bulletin Board

We need to find ways to cut through our excuses and get ourselves into overdrive.

> *"It is not the mountain we conquer, but ourselves"*
> Sir Edmund Hillary

The cornerstone of achieving more is, as Steven R. Covey says, putting 'first things first'. Think about what you really want (or have) to do – you know in your heart what it is – and commit yourself to doing it. Don't give in to the ubiquitous little voice that tries to put you off. Make yourself do it if you have to, and reward yourself when you've done it. It will build your self esteem, confidence and career. You will be doing the right things first. Too few of us do.

Business sense

UK entrepreneurial dynamo, Dr Chris Evans, a rare academic who has been instrumental in the creation and development of several of the UK's most successful biotechnology companies, says: 'Fast growth companies (and people) need the following ingredients – focus, cohesion, simplicity, pace, conviction, enterprise . . . and greatness.'

In the business world there is no greater need for focus and commitment of people than when they are in a merger situation. Reflecting the theme of the personal aspects of change covered in these pages, Mark Feldman and Michael Spratt, the authors of *Five*

Frogs on a Log: A Guide to Mergers, Acquisitions and Gut-wrenching Change, say (unsurprisingly) that the key elements of successful corporate change are speed, focus and momentum.

They argue that navigating such a major transition is a race against time, with years of deployment decisions being made in days, where everything becomes a priority and coping with personal and corporate change is almost overwhelming.

Their recipe for corporate success in these circumstances involves:

- *Focusing* resources and creating *momentum* to develop early wins for shareholders.
- Communicating effectively to stabilise staff and get them *directed.*
- *Seizing* opportunities to make sure resources are in line with the business priorities.
- *Minimising* the distraction and disruption that can cripple production in the early days.

A survey by consultants at Pricewaterhouse-Coopers asked top management of acquirers what they would do differently if they could start again. Nearly 9 out of 10 said they would have acted more quickly in the transition, made more decisions and got more things done. "Perhaps the greatest corporate sin" they concluded, "is moving too slowly to capture the value in the deal."

A good example in action is that of VTEL and Compression Labs in the US. When the two organisations merged to bring the hottest technology to the videoconferencing market, CEO Dick Moeller, insisted that they focus on just two criteria: financial impact and probability of success. They applied the 80/20 rule and identified the 20% of actions likely to drive 80% of the economic value with the highest probability of success. All available resources – time, management and capital – were committed first to the key value-creating priorities.

Talking of commitment, the story of Professor Robert Swan, the first man ever to walk unsupported to both the North and South

Poles, exemplifies the real meaning of commitment, backed by determined action.

> ***"The winners and losers in the 21st century will be distinguished by the speed and quality of the execution – and their commitment to the result"***
> Manoj Badale
> Netdecisions

A fervent environmentalist, Professor Swan was horrified when he arrived at the Antarctic to see the amount of debris left at base camps by previous expeditions, scientific surveys and commercial exploration. He resolved that if, and when, he completed his trek he would return and clear up the mess.

After a harrowing 900 mile journey he made his way back to his polar start point only to discover that his own ship had been crushed by pack ice, leaving him with no choice other than to leave his own 60 tons of equipment there also. He committed to return, but with no money (literally), it took him two full years to raise £526,000 to bring the ship back and enable him and a team to clear up the mess. It would have been easy for him to quietly forget it, but Professor Swan *delivered* on his word.

At the other extreme there are few more action-biased environments than the dot.com world – and perhaps few companies (at the time of writing) exemplify the dot.com mindset more than UK based Lastminute.com the online provider of last-minute offers.

> ***"The challenge for all businesses is to move, and adapt, at 'internet speed'. To change things in a matter of months, not years.***
> Peter Martin
> E-Business Editorial Director, *Financial Times*

Fronted by Brent Hoberman and Martha Lane-Fox, Lastminute spotted a business opportunity and went for it with immense gusto. The key was to see a new market, and to get there first. The site enables consumers to find late bargains ranging from top concert tickets to film premieres and 'once in a lifetime' experiences like a 30 minute flight in a Russian MIG fighter. And on the supplier side, it provides a branded outlet for their spare capacity . . . a cheap way of getting rid of remnants. Lastminute makes its money by taking a cut of each transaction. A simple idea well executed. But is there more to it?

'A lot of people talk', says seasoned internet investor Ricky Tahta. 'Brent doesn't talk. Brent does.'

The question is, do you?

The five 'killer' questions

Am I . . . ?	Yes	No	Maybe
Really focusing my efforts on the right areas for me?			
Doing things that someone else could do instead?			
Setting aside some relaxation time (it can't be all work and no play)			
Putting 'first things first' in my business and home life?			
Rewarding myself for my successes along the way?			
What am I going to do next?			

Focus is obviously linked to goal setting but it shouldn't be a dull and dour grind to 'get there'. Once you've decided what it's best to focus on right now try to give it 100% attention, whether its playing with the kids, talking with your partner, getting that report done or whacking a squash ball around.

You can't effectively focus on more than one thing at any given time, so give yourself a break and give up trying to do the 'impossible'. And make sure you give yourself a reward (it doesn't have to be big!) when you feel you've really achieved something through devoting your full attention to it. It will help to encourage you to build the focus habit.

Chapter 11

Make great decisions, faster

In this chapter . . .

- **Ways to overcome 'paralysis by analysis'**
- **Discover the liberation of 'let's try this'**
- **How to take calculated risks**

An average decision made quickly can have much better results than a good one made slowly – it gives momentum and direction to those making and affected by it. In many leading companies today experimentation is replacing analysis as the decision making process of choice because it works better and results are known quicker.

> ***Our doubts are traitors and make us lose the good we oft might win by fearing to attempt"***
> William Shakespeare

We've all heard the term 'paralysis by analysis' where mounds of research data, followed by further discussion still leaves us in the uncomfortable position of wondering what our action should be. Organisations are getting tired of wasting time 'over-researching' and are keen to do controlled experiments to inform their decisions.

Once again, our educational system is partly to blame for our 'paralysis by analysis' mentality, where there always seemed to be a right and a wrong answer . . . and getting it right was paramount. But in business we never really have enough information on which to base decisions and, even when we do, we promptly find that the goalposts have moved because of some outside factor. Do the analysis, but don't get hung up on it. Make a decision and remember that you can change your mind if it is wrong.

"Do it , fix it , try it is our favourite axiom. In other words, be decisive"
Tom Peters and Robert Waterman
In Search of Excellence

Taking risks and knowing when to cut your losses is the mark of the entrepreneur. Decisions do not normally produce 'right' and 'wrong' answers; it's not as black and white as that. They could be 75% right, or the other way. Whenever you make a decision you can't know for sure what the future holds, so change your mindset and use the phrase 'let's *try* this.'

Try implies experimentation and effort, and acknowledges up front that it may not work. In decision making the goal shouldn't be to avoid failure; as one eminent philosopher said 'If you're not failing occasionally you are not taking enough risks.' If you do blow it, learn from it. It's very releasing to accept that mistakes will be made!

3M, for example, encourages 'scientific playfulness'. Its philosophy is: *When in doubt vary, change, solve the problem, seize the opportunity, experiment, try something new – even if you can't predict precisely how things will turn out. Do something! If one thing fails, try another. Fix, try, do, adjust. Move, act – whatever you do, don't sit still. Vigorous action creates momentum.* Phew!

Peter Drucker, the marketing and business guru, must have had all this in mind when he said, 'People who *don't* take risks generally make about two big mistakes a year. People who *do* take risks generally make about two big mistakes a year.'

"In a life where death is the hunter, my friend, there is no time for fear or regrets – only decisions"
Don Juan

Part of the essence of great decision making is to create your own deadline for making it. It helps to drive your energy, concentrate your mind and prepare yourself for some action. This isn't just theoretical mumbo jumbo – it could have meant the difference between life and death in Northern Ireland, a land where agreement on the correct course of action for peace has been so elusive.

> ***"Be approximately right. Make decisions quickly rather than be precisely right . . . and be left behind"***
> Ian Armitage
> CEO, Mercury Private Equity

Senator George Mitchell, who has already been featured in these pages, has something to say about the critical importance of setting a deadline. Of the Good Friday agreement to make peace possible in Northern Ireland, he said, 'We knew that the existence of a deadline didn't guarantee success, but the absence of a deadline would certainly guarantee failure.'

You don't have to take decisions on your own, of course. Hunt for solutions by brainstorming with colleagues or family members if appropriate. Consult experts in areas outside your knowledge; ask friends for an independent view but, after taking all this into account, the decision you take is your responsibility. That's where it comes back to you, how you approach the choices you make and the direction you take.

And don't forget your intuition, your 'gut feel' based on your knowledge and experience. 'Does it feel right' is a good test of the soundness of your decision.

Bulletin Board

Decisions in business and life are rarely right and wrong. What is often more important than the decision itself is how it is seen through, and how the actions needed to ensure a successful outcome are implemented.

> ***"The higher up you go the more mistakes you are allowed. Right at the top if you make enough of them it is considered to be your style"***
> Fred Astaire

The immense amount of data available to support our decisions these days does not always help us to clarify

matters. On the contrary, on occasions we are bamboozled by the many facets of an issue presented to us. Ultimately, we should recognise that decisions are made as a 'snapshot' in time, the world changes and we must adapt.

Good decision making requires the characteristics of 'review' that we saw in goal setting so that the course can be altered to meet the changing circumstances in which our decisions are made.

Business sense

As Subhir Chowdhury, author of *Management 21C* says:

> '*Believe* . . . that should be the 21st century leader's watchword. There is a big difference between accepting and believing. Leaders must create an atmosphere in which people *believe* in the strategy, believe in the management's decisions and believe in their work. Once people believe in management decisions there is a palpable excitement within an organisation.'

And, as Jack Welch, GE's veteran chairman, said: 'We want people who get up every morning with a passion about finding a better way; finding for their associates in the office, finding from another company or another market. We are constantly on the search, and feeling our way.'

> *"Increasingly, the companies that win are those who learn faster, act quicker and adapt sooner. They compress time by making, and executing early, informed decisions about economic value creation, ruthless prioritisation and focused resource allocation"*
> Mark Feldman

Jack's tone suggests that there is a lot of trial and error at GE, that they tolerate 'good, but not quite good enough' tries. It's the same sort of mentality demonstrated by the organisations in Tom Peters' and Robert Waterman's famous (or infamous) *In Search of Excellence*, where the leaders of the day emphasised the need to focus on the customer and the changes in the market. In other words to be quick about doing something if you feel it is right, but keep an eagle eye on it in case you were wrong, and change direction accordingly.

Michael Jackson, chairman of UK stock market darling Sage Group Plc and of venture capital provider Elderstreet Investments, describes key moments in an organisation's fortunes as 'hinge factors', where decisions taken can change the whole course of the business.

In the early 1980s Sage, a supplier of accounting and payroll software to small and medium sized businesses, had hit a plateau in its performance, and was going nowhere . . . until the introduction of Alan Sugar's low-cost Amstrad computer opened up a potential market opportunity – Sage made the decision to 'have a go' and to grab it with both hands.

> ***"Those who are victorious plan effectively and change decisively. They are like a great river that maintains its course but adjusts its flow"***
> Sun Tsu
> Chinese war strategist

Developing new software marketed at a rock bottom price, Sage appealed to the small business person who wanted to manage their own business and financial affairs. The product took off, and Sage, from having just four founder members based in Newcastle in north-east England in 1981, now has a FTSE 100 stock market listing with a market capitalisation of over £8.5bn and employs over 4,000 people.

Michael, in his role as a venture capitalist, also advocates the value of seeing the 'hinge factor' in decision making. 'It's not always easy to make tough decisions, particularly when there's not enough information, or you are relying on your instinct', he says. 'But I've seen the fortunes of businesses change immeasurably though being brave with your decision making. If things, or people, need to change, change them.'

> ***"We moved rapidly even at the risk of making some mistakes. And we don't seem to have made any more mistakes than if we had taken twice as long"***
> Jeremy Strachan
> Glaxo (on the merger with Wellcome)

It sounds simple enough, but there are

still too many organisations out there who want certainty before they act. The only problem with such an over-analytical and ponderous process is that the Lord Mayor's show has passed on by the time they've decided to take their place. Hope you and your organisation have a better view.

The five 'killer' questions

Am I . . . ?	Yes	No	Maybe
Stuck in the right/wrong mode of decision making?			
Making decisions fast enough?			
Backing my decisions with massive action to maximise the likelihood of success?			
Enlisting the help of others where they can add value?			
Making a habit of reviewing my decisions so that I can see what has happened as a result and can be clear about what to do next?			
What am I going to do next?			

If you are a slow decision maker, whilst it may be difficult at first to get out of your usual way of making decisions, persevere with the feeling of 'risk' which comes with quickly plumping for a certain course. Taking action to ensure the best possible outcome from your decision is the greatest antidote to worrying about whether it was right or wrong.

Chapter 12

Super-productive meetings in half the time

In this chapter . . .

- **Are your meetings teamwork generators or time wasters?**
- **Five ways to protect yourself from meeting overload**
- **Golden rules to make sure you squeeze full value from your meetings**

A one hour long meeting each day, occupying four people with an average salary of £25,000 will cost you at least £35,000 a year. And that's without calculating the loss of the other more productive things that those people could have been doing.

Meetings are great ways to pass on information, solve problems, brainstorm ideas and motivate your team. They can also be a complete waste of time. Organising, travelling to, and participating in meetings can form a huge chunk of an executive's working week. But anyone who attends such gatherings regularly will agree that many shouldn't be held at all. Bad meetings are a massive drain on resources and money, but properly run ones can achieve wonders. How can you make sure that yours do?

There's no secret to the basics, but many of us forget them in the hurly burly of our daily schedules. Let's recap.

- Send an agenda in advance, covering:
  - The objectives of the meeting
  - The points to be covered and the discussion time allocated to each
  - The start and finish times and location of the meeting

- Protect your time – from a personal perspective ask yourself these five questions:
  1. What is the point of the meeting?
  2. Why am I attending?
  3. What can I contribute?
  4. Am I the best/right person to go?
  5. How can I get the most out of it in the least time?

The aim should always be to get the minimum number of the right people present. Whilst cutting down numbers is not always easy due to the politics concerned, meetings of more than ten rarely achieve the pace and motivation you are seeking from a powerful session. Four or five people can often achieve a good deal more.

Never doubt that a small group of thoughtful, committed people can change the world. Indeed, it is the only thing that ever has.

If yours is an organisation that has 'big' meetings, one way to encourage smaller numbers is to invite only the essential players, but to send a note to all the other interested parties with the agenda stating that they are welcome to attend *if* they have something specific to contribute on a particular agenda item.

This approach weeds out those who would have attended just to be seen to be involved. Everyone in the meeting room should have a positive reason for being there, and be in a position to participate effectively and make decisions.

Complete the circle of communication by sending the action points from the meeting to those individuals originally circulated with the agenda, in addition to the participants in the meeting itself. In this way colleagues won't feel isolated and will be kept fully in the picture on important decisions taken.

> ***"A meeting's productivity is inversely proportionate to the number of people attending it"***
> Mark McCormack

Make sure that all essential or long papers are circulated well in advance of the meeting; and create a culture which expects the participants to have read them beforehand, not at the meeting!

The knack of creating great meetings is having a leader who does the basics in advance and keeps the proceedings moving. If you are chairing make it a policy to start on time and emphasise this fact politely to latecomers – they won't do it again. Don't waste the meeting participant's time either, stamp on anything trivial and move it 'outside the meeting'. On the other hand be flexible on timing if real progress on a 'meaty' issue is being made.

If you are a participant you also have a responsibility for making the meeting run smoothly. Follow the rules laid down by the chairman. Many a meeting is 'hijacked' by one individual who insists on monopolising the discussion. They get away with it simply because the other attendees allow them to.

Never allow interruptions to the meeting unless absolutely necessary. The momentum can quickly evaporate if participants leave to answer mobile phones or deal with messages passed through by secretaries.

Urgency concentrates the mind. A meeting scheduled an hour before lunch or late in the afternoon can be rattled through because participants' mindsets are right – they recognise that they have limited time for discussion, and getting to the point is easier.

Set some ground rules of openness, frankness and confidentiality for your team meetings – the 'anything goes but it stays within these four walls' approach. To keep the momentum, if you have to eat do it while you are discussing, but make sure you do allow time for a laugh and a joke – there's no substitute for face to face interaction to build team spirit, and nobody said meetings have to be dull, boring affairs!

Meetings are usually called to make decisions. Make sure any commitments made in your meetings are clear, and that participants go away knowing precisely what to do. Talk, without constructive follow up action is usually wasted time.

Do a quick 'round table ' update on opportunities and issues at the end of your meetings. People agree to do things that would not have surfaced otherwise. Make sure these actions are captured in the minutes.

Getting together regularly (e.g. weekly) as a team can be very time efficient – particularly if you have a rule where your people save up their non-urgent problems for the meeting. It clears your diary, which can often be blocked by such time-wasting discussions during the rest of the week.

Weekly meetings are also superb for keeping your people 'on vision' . . . whatever your goals may be. Simply ask your people to address these two questions:

- What *have I done* to help us move closer to our goals
- What *am I going to do* this week to move us closer to our goals

In no time at all you'll have your team members thinking on the Wednesday before your Friday meeting 'what can I say this week, what *have* I done to help us move closer to our goals.' You wouldn't get anywhere near the same level of ownership of the vision if you didn't regularly ask the questions.

> ***"The management challenge of the Millennium is to get ordinary people to do extraordinary things. Enthusiasm is the match that lights the fuse"***
> Allan Leighton
> Chief Executive
> ASDA Stores

Make sure that whoever is capturing the action points for the meeting circulates them as quickly as possible – the same day is by far the best – it shows urgency and the importance you attach to the actions. Ensure that they cover who has committed to do what, and by when. There's no need for a full regurgitation of the discussion, just concentrate on the actions.

To complete the virtuous circle and really get things moving in your organisation, challenge people rigorously if they haven't done the things they committed to do by the due date (and that's another reason to get the action points out quickly); otherwise you will constantly be dealing with excuses and covering 'old ground' ...and your meetings will be in danger of falling into the 'nothing ever happens' category. Encourage the peer pressure that the 'rule' is to complete your agreed actions by the meeting.

Following the simple keys to running effective meetings ensures that people come charged up for a powerful and productive session.

Bulletin Board

Despite modern technology, meetings are still going to be the normal way for colleagues to get together to discuss issues and opportunities, forge team spirit and to communicate.

They are so much a part of many peoples' working lives that we forget how much time and money each meeting actually costs. Whilst we all know instinctively what makes for a good meeting, the vast majority do not stick to the basic rules of timeliness and keeping to the point.

The 'housekeeping' work of circulating information in advance (and expecting everyone to have read the papers before the meeting) and preparing clear minutes identifying who has agreed to do what, by when, prepares the ground for a great meeting. There is nothing difficult in this, all that is required is good business discipline so that meetings are seen to be a platform for decision making and momentum, not a 'talking shop' where no one around the table sees its value.

Critically review the meetings you attend. How could they be improved? Then ask yourself the most important

question of all – do you really need the meeting and, if so, do *you* have to be there?

Business sense

ASDA, the UK retailing giant bought by Wal-Mart of the US, embodies the principles of having super-productive meetings in half the time: they do it by having no chairs in the meeting rooms!

Seriously, they have waist high 'tables' where meeting attendees stand to discuss the issues on the agenda. The physical act of standing creates the urgency and focus required to 'get to the point' and concentrate on the matters at hand. There's no leaning back on chairs, hands behind head, pontificating. There's no ceremonial pouring of tea. Instead you get a dynamic meeting of equals, sharp discussion and quick decisions. It's a tremendous approach.

Here's another thought. How much time could be saved if your organisation *really* focused on holding meetings for only those matters critical to the business – and even then kept the numbers actually attending to the bare minimum.

That's exactly what US based Co-operative Systems did when it acquired rival Triad Systems. CEO Glenn Staats built his new teams around the 80/20 principle, that 20% of the actions taken are likely to drive 80% of the value. Good, but so far so ordinary.

This is the really interesting point. Because he believed that a team of more than five people has difficulty simply scheduling its next meeting (how true) most teams were small. And no teams were formed around actions best left to competent individuals.

Does this happen in your organisation. If not, why not?

The five 'killer' questions

Am I . . . ?	Yes	No	Maybe
Running my own meetings in line with these 'best practice' ideas?			

Attending any meetings where my time could be spent better elsewhere?			
Contributing fully to those I do attend (including reading all the papers beforehand)?			
Great at completing the actions I agree at meetings?			
Using technology to the full to minimise the time and cost of meetings?			
What am I going to do next?			

Perhaps issuing a one-pager with your own ground rules for meetings is the way to reinforce the message to your people that you want short, pithy, action-oriented discussions. Poor meetings cost you money, good ones can create a platform for making it.

If you can't get face to face try videoconferencing or conference calls with a time limit. It's often amazing how much you can get through if everyone is prepared and plays the game by the 'good meeting' ground rules.

Where am I now?

Success Secret No. 3, make things happen, involves three keys; creating a compelling vision of what you want to achieve (through goal setting) committing to doing it (through strengthening your 'do it' muscle) and taking fast and decisive action (by achieving more in less time). Making things happen is the engine room of your success; it's what most people see because action is tangible. Are you seen as an action dynamo?

So far we've adapted to change, we've given our creativity and mental capacity a shot in the arm, and now we're really moving fast.

Let's make sure that we mentally and physically stay on track . . .

Barefoot on broken glass

Walking on the 2,000 pieces of broken glass needs the physical application of all of the disciplines covered in this section. Getting to the other side unharmed is the compelling vision, committing to doing it means stepping boldly forward, and focusing on one step at a time whilst keeping the end goal in mind.

Nothing happens until you take the first step!

If you are interested in free, more detailed goal setting, visualisation and 'just do it' stuff, visit the website at ***www.barefootbook.com****.*

Secret 4

Create the 2001 attitude

"Do not be too timid and squeamish about your actions. All life is an experiment"
Ralph Waldo Emerson

Chapter 13

Practical positive thinking

In this chapter . . .

- **The benefits of 'feet on the ground' positive thinking**
- **Techniques to 'tune out' the negativity around you**
- **Five ways to decide to have a good day**
- **Learn to recognise the 'downers' of life and move past them**

We have all read books and articles about the power of positive thinking, and agreed that thinking more positively can, indeed, improve our lives. The only problem is that positive thinking as proposed by some authorities is almost impossible to live up to. When things get tough for us our positive thoughts are likely to fly straight out of the window, and it needs a strong will to coax them back in!

> ***"The greatest discovery of my generation is that a human being can alter his life by altering his attitude of mind"***
> William James

Those of us who are into positive thinking may be setting unrealistic expectations of ourselves by aiming to think positively all the time, and we are deflated when we don't live up to our own standards. Given that we are constantly bombarded with negative messages (just listen to a news broadcast or read a national newspaper; negative messages *make* the news) it's no wonder that situations sometimes get us down.

Perhaps our start point should be to think 'not negative' and to accept that we do sometimes have negative thoughts, instead of beating ourselves up because we've let some slip through our guard. It doesn't mean that we have to be guided by them, or give into them, it simply means that we can observe our negative thoughts and let them go. Giving ourselves permission to accept that we are not going to be 'perfectly positive' all the time is very releasing and practical.

"Results! Why man, I've gotten a lot of results. I know several thousand things that won't work"
Thomas Edison

Your aim should be to learn from what is happening, good and bad, and to be mindful of the many negative messages fed to us (and those we feed ourselves in our daily lives). Listen to them but deliberately turn down the volume, and make the decision not to be swept along by the feeling. It's natural to worry from time to time, to be uncertain, upset, depressed or fearful on occasions, so don't deny the feelings. If you fail in thinking positively at these times, don't let it get you down. The next thought you have is your opportunity to start again and move forward.

Our thoughts and how we deal with them are what make our days and life successful or not, happy or miserable. They can limit our creativity and problem solving, or liberate us to explore new ways of doing things. Our thoughts drive our feelings, moods and well-being just as surely as a steering wheel drives a car. They can, and do, create our own heaven or hell.

"Attitudes are more important than facts"
Dr Karl Meninger

Most of us, however, take too much notice of our negative thoughts and give scant attention to *creating* our own encouraging messages. Sure, we all have good and bad days, but training our thoughts can really help to minimise the 'off days' and create the 'feel goods' much more often.

Without a conscious effort we tend to entertain any old thought that happens to wander into our mind. To be practically positive we need to 'tune out' the negative thoughts – just let them drift past – and instead 'lock onto' to more positive ones that will enhance our lives and those of others we come into contact with.

> ***"The real secret of success is enthusiasm"***
> Walter Chrysler

Make no mistake, this takes constant practice, but it gets easier as the positivity habit develops. It means exercising your 'positive muscle' and letting the negative one wither so that it can have less of a grip on you. Notice your thoughts; what do they tell you about yourself and your present attitude?

To summarise so far, we *do* have control over what we think. We can *decide* to have a good day, to ignore that remark, to reject our own negative thoughts and replace them with more helpful ones. Indeed, we have to control them because, as we all know, one negative thought quickly leads to another. Don't let the downward spiral happen, decide *in advance* what your positive thoughts should be, and recall them when you feel yourself 'going negative'. Try these to get you going:

1. What are you most proud of about yourself or your family?
2. What's your favourite tune? (Hum or sing it to give you a really practical lift . . . go on try it!)
3. Recall your goals and dreams. (What do you *really* want out of your life?)
4. Remember when someone complimented you.
5. 'See' a positive outcome to the thing you are doing, or are going to do next.

Practical positive thinking is like exercise, you need to work at it regularly, but the results can really change your life. Have fun, play with creative questions to focus positive thoughts which can guide your actions and help you to do things you would never normally have done. For example:

- What can I do to make this the best week of my life?

- What can I do to make this a special evening/weekend for my partner?
- How can I make some positive use out of this flight/train delay or traffic jam, etc.?

Focus on the big things that will enhance your life, don't waste time fretting over trivial matters. The chances are that you can't even remember what you were worrying about last week. Have a go and, if that's true, why worry or get upset in the first place? It can't have been that bad!

> ***"Man is born a Stradivarius but raised to believe he is a fiddle"***
> Jean Huston

Our success in life depends on how we set our minds. The brain follows the principles of Gestalt and attempts to actualise our thoughts. If we think it's going to be a bad day, our brain will set to work to create one for us . . . and give us many reasons to support our conviction. Thankfully the reverse is also true. Ask yourself 'How can I do (whatever it is you want)?' and your brain will set to work seeking creative ways to help you to achieve your wishes. The obvious moral is to focus on what we want, not on what we wish to avoid.

Here are some fun techniques to keep you positive. Notice how similar some of them are to the 'exaggeration' techniques of memory enhancement and mind mapping, it's the language the brain understands best.

> ***"If you are distressed by anything external, the pain is not due to the thing itself but to your estimate of it – and this you have the power to revoke at any moment"***
> Marcus Aurelius
> (AD 120–180)

When you are worried, try this . . .

Sit quietly and see yourself writing out all your concerns on separate pieces of paper. Then set fire to them, either individually or all in one go. Warm your hands on them, see your face glow in the light of the warmth created . . . laugh and let go. Doesn't that feel better!

Keep smiling!

The physical act of smiling helps us to feel better. Give it your best shot, smile at everyone you meet – be crazy, put a skip in your step and energy in your body even if you don't feel like it, act it. You'll look and feel better, and the difference in your attitude and that of the people around you will be amazing.

Quote, unquote

Choose your favourite motivational phrases from this book and others and write them down. All the best performers do this, from top salespeople to leading business figures and actors. Put them somewhere handy and refer to them often. They'll change your mood and mindset quicker than any pill.

Share a joke

People love to laugh, so why don't you be the catalyst? Learn a joke, or a one liner if jokes aren't your forte (or is this just a comfort zone thing?). Be someone who brings a laugh into other people's lives.

Enjoy life

Take time to see the things around you, smell your partner's perfume, see your child's smile, accept your colleague's compliment. Don't be so hell bent on reaching your destination that you forget to enjoy the scenery on the way. The small, day-to-day things aren't just the building blocks of life, they are it! And, as John Lennon once remarked, 'Life is what happens to us while we're making other plans.'

> ***"Plunge into the thick of life"***
> Goethe

Focus on the end result

Don't get discouraged along the way. Set your sights on the victory of the completed task. That's how long-distance runners, mountain climbers and arctic explorers motivate themselves, by focusing on the sense of relief, achievement and exhilaration when to goal is reached. That's exactly the technique used by polar explorer Professor Robert Swan. Not easy at –70°C and pulling 365lb!

Celebrate your successes

We've all done something we are proud of, it doesn't have to be big. Think of all your achievements, large and small. They needn't be academic, and don't put yourself down if you are not; we all have skills and abilities unique to us. Celebrate your complexity – our bodies are miraculous structures that even the best doctors and scientists are only beginning to understand, and the brain of each and everyone of us is far more sophisticated than the biggest and best computer we can build. We've got a lot to be proud of before we even start!

> ***"There is only one success – to be able to spend your life in your own way"***
> Christopher Morley

Avoid the downers of life

What are the things which really get us depressed and set off the trains of negative thoughts that tend to take us lower and lower? Most of them are 'feelings' like:

- Not being appreciated
- Not being listened to
- Life's unfair
- We are not loved
- We are jealous
- Being humiliated
- Being ignored
- Being overwhelmed
- Being betrayed
- Being envious

> ***"The secret of success is a real passion for what you are doing. Whatever it is, enjoy it"***
> Richard Branson

- Being worried
- Being tired

We all have these feelings to varying degrees at one time or another. Notice how many of them can be brought about by the changes covered in the first section of this book. No wonder we feel stressed if change hits us hard! It can start a downward spiral of unhelpful emotions that need to be nipped in the bud.

It's important is to recognise the emotion for what it is and move on, ideally to replace it in your mind with a positive feeling through one of the techniques highlighted earlier. We have the power to develop the counterbalance to these and create positive feelings for ourselves and others. All we need to do is to use the techniques to 'tune into' a more positive train of thought and help us to feel:

- Appreciated and praised
- Good about our achievements
- Good about ourselves
- Motivated and inspired
- Recognised for our efforts
- Healthy, happy and successful
- Loving and kind
- Proud of ourselves and others

You'll recognise, of course, that these are some of the feelings we came across in the very first exercise on 'What do we want more of' (page 2).

Bulletin Board

Almost everyone agrees with the philosophy of positive thinking, but few of us really take it seriously and build it into our lives. We listen, read and nod sagely, hoping that knowledge alone will carry us through – it won't. As usual, it requires action, it needs us to choose to be positive and

"If you ask what I have come to do in this world . . . I will repy I'm here to live my life OUT LOUD"
Emile Zola

to decide what the things are that will make our day, week or year. It's up to us; we can choose our goals and dreams and make them happen with small steps each day, celebrating progress as we go, and enjoying the moment. Or we can choose a life of negative emotions. It's our decision because our thoughts run the show.

The five 'killer' questions

Am I . . . ?	Yes	No	Maybe
A prime example of 'practical' positive thinking?			
Choosing to programme my thoughts to be positive ones?			
Suffering from any of the 'downers' of life right now?			
'Tuning out' negative thoughts when they strike?			
Using my skills to help others feel more positive about themselves?			
What am I going to do next?			

Many of us find it easier to focus on negative rather than positive feelings. Maybe we are just made that way, or perhaps it's become a habit. Changing the way we think takes time, but it's worth the effort. Make a point of trying to see a different viewpoint on those thoughts and emotions that tend to bring you 'down'.

You can often proactively avoid those situations where we create our own stress. The next chapter will give you the key . . .

Chapter 14

The golden 15 minutes

In this chapter . . .

- **A 15 minute cushion that could change your life**
- **Learn to be still, with one of five exercises**
- **How to keep your peak mental and physical performance**

> ***"I'm late, I'm late for a very important date. No time to say hello, goodbye. I'm late, I'm late, I'm late"***
> *From Alice in Wonderland*

We often create our own time pressures and stress by forgetting to build enough 'contingency' time in our day. We never seem to have enough time, from the moment we get out of bed, rush our breakfast, jump into the car or go for the bus or train. Our need to finish one task at work leads us to be late for our meeting, and at the end of it all we dash home hoping that our partner won't realise that we are, once again, 15 minutes late. We have spent the whole day chasing our tail. Does this sound like you?

No wonder that you fall into bed exhausted, only to repeat the process the very next day. You simply have to break the habit!

The answer is to create a 'cushion' of time for yourself – a golden 15 minutes which can change your days from stressful to stress-free. A cushion is soft, it feels good, it is relaxing . . . here's how you can do it with a little self-discipline.

> ***"Next week there can't be a crisis, my schedule is already full"***
> Henry Kissinger

Start by creating your 15 minute cushion by getting up quarter of an hour earlier in the morning. You can use it for a number of things, as we'll see, but one of the key things is to give you enough time to do things without constantly feeling under pressure. It will also give you enough time to focus on your goals and the actions you can take to reach them.

Here are 20 things you can do with your golden 15 minutes

1. Review your 'to do' lists and the day ahead.
2. Use it to meditate or visualise and set yourself up for the day (some ways to do it are given later).
3. Exercise. Studies have shown that just 15 minutes of vigorous exercise three times a week will keep you fit and healthy.
4. Set off to work 15 minutes early, miss the rush and arrive relaxed.
5. Leave work 15 minutes early and delight and surprise your partner!
6. Arrive early for meetings (and use the time to do the small bits of paperwork you never have time to do).
7. Call a friend just to keep in touch (it's important to maintain your relationships).
8. Write a letter – maybe even to your partner (you romantic thing!).
9. Practice your speed reading techniques (15 minutes is all it takes).
10. Develop your memory (a quarter hour is just enough each day).

11. Think about your goals and dreams, and what small steps you need to take next.
12. Create a mind map (you can easily do one in 15 minutes) to help you solve a problem or 'brainstorm' an opportunity.
13. Spend a quality 15 minutes with your children and/or partner, just listening and talking (the rewards are immense!).
14. Set aside 15 minutes to review any information you need to retain (remember, review your notes properly and it'll be locked in there for as long as you wish).
15. Listen to motivational tapes to keep your emotions positive, and give yourself a boost.
16. Share a joke with your friends.
17. Say a prayer or two to your God, and focus on how you can make an even better contribution today.
18. Pay your household bills (an important task before it becomes urgent).
19. Plan how you will make the most of the coming weekend.
20. Relax and visualise yourself being the person you've always wanted to be, doing the things you've always wanted to do!

One of the best ways of relaxing, sparking your creativity and generally getting in tune with yourself is to sit for 15 minutes literally 'doing nothing'. Some call it meditation, others label it as visualisation. Dr Herbert Benson (whose book the *Relaxation Response* was a revelation in its day) sees it as a physical body relaxation thing.

Whatever your views, everyone from Zen Buddhists through to positive thinkers believe that sitting quietly for a short period is very restorative and powerful. The self-discipline involved in carving out the time is hard enough for many of us. Add to that the discipline of doing what we are asked to do to fulfil the ritual of the relaxation we are following and it's a major achievement.

Just the act of regularly doing the meditation/visualisation probably goes a long way towards its success in helping us to

"Act as though it were impossible to fail"
Emile Coue

become more focused and relaxed. There are plenty of references at the back of the book for relaxation and meditation techniques. Why not experiment and find one that suits you? If you've never done it before here's a few approaches to try:

Method one

Sweep your body with your attention, starting at the top of your head and moving down your body, concentrating on each part as you go, and allowing it to relax.

Method two

Tense your body as hard as you can. Clench your fists, curl your toes, tighten your biceps and buttocks, screw up your face. Hold the tension for a few seconds to experience how it feels, then let go and relax completely. Exhale your breath and notice the difference. Repeat the exercise a couple of times.

Method three

"There is more to life than increasing its speed"
Mahatma Ghandi

Take five slow breaths and aim to breathe slowly and smoothly afterwards with no breaks between breaths. Visualise the flow of relaxation as you talk to yourself saying slowly 'my feet are relaxed . . . my ankles, knees and hips feel heavy, relaxed and comfortable. My stomach, chest and back feel beautifully relaxed and quiet. My hands feel warm and relaxed, my neck, jaw, face and forehead are all beautifully free, comfortable and smooth . . . I feel totally serene and calm.

Method four

Concentrate on your breathing and let your mind become as calm and even as the natural rhythm of your breathing. Observe whatever thoughts arise without getting involved with them, just let them bubble up and float off.

Method five

Imagine that a turquoise coloured mist of relaxation and well-being surrounds you. When you breathe in, imagine the mist filling your head, neck and shoulders, sinking into every pore. Breathing out, visualise all the tension and strain which are present in that area going out with the mist. Breathe the mist in again, concentrate on your chest, and breathe out all the tension. Repeat for all parts of the body.

At the other end of the spectrum to the process of sitting still and meditating is working the body through exercise. Most people are aware that physical exercise produces endorphins in the brain, the body's own pain relieving and tension busting chemical.

In the West, however, we are a largely sedentary society – recent reports say that over half of the UK population is overweight – and the thought of exercise repels many of us. We pretend it doesn't and even go as far as joining health clubs, buying weights, exercise cycles or the latest paraphernalia designed to get us fit in the quickest possible time with least effort. But we usually give up after the first flush of activity – there are all sorts of reasons why, but mostly it's just that we don't really have the motivation or desire to get (or remain) fit, it hurts too much, we have to try too hard . . . we head back to comfort.

It takes courage to push yourself to places you have never been before – to test your limits – to break through your barriers

It's your choice whether you want to get fit or not, but physical fitness is a superb platform for doing things. Medical and psychological studies highlight that if we are fit we've got more energy, feel better about ourselves and live longer. We all know this – but why then are the newspaper classified advertisement columns filled with 'as new' exercise equipment for sale?

Bulletin Board

We can all create a quarter hour each day, no matter how busy we are. Using the golden 15 minutes as a cushion can transform how we run our daily lives, so too can using it pro-actively to create the life we want; to learn, to love and take the small amount of time we need to connect with ourselves and others.

You can do all we have covered in this book to make your life more purposeful, productive and fun; the secret is the golden 15 minutes and your willingness to devote the time required to change the way you do things.

To survive and thrive in the new Millennium you need to rely on the wealth of attributes you already possess. You are only using a tiny percentage of your ability at present, but your potential is huge. It's just sat there waiting to be tapped into for the benefit of you and others.

Business sense

There have been countless studies which show that relaxation and meditation can have a profound effect on individual wellbeing, creativity and focus. Studies have also been carried out at the organisational level where teams, or entire workforces, have been trained in one technique or another. Transcendental meditation is one approach that has been the subject of more than its fair share of analyses.

The results prove conclusively that those organisations where their people practised focused resting, visualisation and taking time out for themselves performed measurably better than the 'control' organisations that didn't.

Whilst some of the 'soft' measures like better health, greater harmony and improved communication might not cut too much ice with some, these translated to the 'bottom line' in the form of less absenteeism, greater productivity, and improved sales (attributed to better teamwork and sharing of ideas). Now that's worth sitting thinking about!

In a nutshell, happier, more relaxed people perform better and can more easily create the passion, drive, energy and enthusiasm that all organisations pray their people will have. Thinking about your people and helping them to manage their mindset could be the best investment you ever make.

The five 'killer' questions

Am I . . . ?	Yes	No	Maybe
Good at creating a 'cushion' of time in the day?			
Spending enough time relaxing?			
Using my 'golden 15 minutes' to the greatest effect?			
Exercising regularly enough?			
Spending enough time with my loved ones?			
What am I going to do next?			

The 'cushion' idea really works if you keep it constantly in mind. Why not put a Post-It note on your desk, in the car or on the bathroom mirror until it is ingrained in your subconscious. The key is to maintain the cushion throughout the day. If it dwindles try to take a few moments to analyse why, but don't beat yourself up if you didn't make it last, there's always another chance tomorrow.

It's one of the best, and simplest, time management ideas going.

Where am I now?

Success Secret No. 4 is to create the 2001 attitude, a way of thinking that is positive yet realistic, and reflects the mood of our time. Your mental and physical well-being overlays the other secrets of success – thriving on change, releasing your potential and, simply, 'going for it'.

But there's more. Whilst squeezing the most out of the present you need to keep one eye on the future.

You may have been lucky enough to have had the joy of playing in the sea by the shore, running in the surf and oblivious to what's going on around you when, from nowhere, comes a wave much bigger and stronger than the others. See it in time and you can have great fun riding it, or run away whooping with the excitement of it all.

If you are taken unawares, however, when the 'big breaker' hits you it's a shocking and altogether more unpleasant experience.

It's the same with change in the business world today. You need to see the big waves coming . . .

Barefoot on broken glass

You cannot walk on broken glass without injury if you are unprepared. Willpower alone won't get you across – it's not as simple as that. To achieve the feat you need to have the right attitude, a calm self-belief, a quiet mind, the inner feeling that you want to do it, and to accept the risks. Critically, you also need to have due respect for the glass.

This attitude is like the one displayed by the real 'greats' of any endeavour; business and sport are the highest profile arenas, but there are many more, where the true leaders really understand themselves and their role . . . they display a mixture of charisma and visionary thinking.

Secret 5

Seeing the big picture

"For years corporate chairmen have been talking about their people as their primary assets. . . . It's about time they woke up to the fact that it's actually true, because their only hope for future security lies in the brains of those people"
Charles Handy

Chapter 15

Ride the mega-waves of change

In the 21st century, the long-term success of organisations will depend to a large extent on their ability to leverage human and intellectual capital. That is, to make the most of you and me.

Their greatest challenge is managing – or adapting to – the pace and simultaneity of economic, demographic, technological and other changes in order to create truly effective people and organisations.

There are several 'waves of change' going on around us all the time, but seeing the big picture involves getting above the mêlée of activity and observing the big 'breakers'. I think these are the ones effective people and organisations should consider. They are making our future, right now.

Big breaker 1: industry convergence

Consolidation – the combination of entities in like industries – was the watchword of the 1980s and 1990s. All that's changed now and consolidation has given way to convergence, driven by changing relations between businesses and their customers. Convergence is blurring the boundaries that once kept businesses apart, and is redefining countless industries and markets.

So what's happened all of a sudden? People have got the hang of IT, and the internet is bringing a nearly limitless number of sales channels into every office and home. This two-way electronic pipeline not only enables businesses to reach far more customers than ever before, it also gives them the means to tell businesses what they want, to love them if they do, and to reject those who don't. Customers (business to business or consumer) are accelerating convergence by compelling businesses to repackage products and services into new offerings.

A great example is the fact that all of the world's stock markets will be linked very soon. Global trading for the personal as well as the corporate investor will be as simple as switching on the computer. Do you want to buy shares on the Japanse, US or European markets – instantly? You can . . . and automatically choose the market that will give you the best price. Why? Because the consumer wants it that way. The individual Stock Exchanges have no option but to meet the demands of customers otherwise they will not survive.

As John T. Wall, President of the US technology stock market NASDAQ, puts it: 'You can't hide very long today before a customer says 'get it for me quicker and cheaper." Money has no passport and no loyalty. Money goes where the best deal is.'

"In business it used to be the big eating the small. Now it's the fast eating the slow"
Chairman
Cisco Systems

The web offers massive opportunity to companies that can change. To others it poses significant threat. Its limitless channels are a godsend for sellers – but they also let buyers search those channels with ease for the products and services they want, at prices they are willing to pay.

The successful companies in converging industries are likely to be the ones who take pre-emptive strikes to seize the opportunity and neutralise the threat.

They'll be redefining their approach to winning business, moving away from selling a single product to undifferentiated legions, to capturing a limited set of individual customers and selling them packages tailored to exactly what they want. They'll also be fully exploiting customer data, understanding customer trends much better, and using it to change what they offer.

The Internet, with its unprecedented ability to capture customer behaviour is, of course, a rich vein of info, but savvy companies will also pay much closer attention to more traditional sources of information such as point of sale data, stored in and later extracted from conventional data warehouses.

Naturally tomorrow's winners will have to become more agile and flexible, and keep a sharper eye on core competencies – the things they do best and the areas where they make the most money.

Succeeding in the era of converging industries means being able to quickly redefine your business and keep in line with customer needs. You'll need to refocus capital away from non core activities and use technology to not only communicate more quickly with suppliers and vendors, but to establish strategic alliances with business partners that add value up and down the supply chain.

Finally, and here's where the human element kicks in hard, successful companies in converging industries must be led by courageous decision makers who are on top of their markets, understand their customers; and have the vision to know when even successful businesses need to redefine themselves. And, of course, they must have the courage to act on that knowledge – because their competitors surely will.

Big breaker 2: e-business

It won't be long before the 'e' in e-business is gone. It's inevitable. Electronic business will quickly evolve to such an extent, and its impact on business will be so pervasive, there will be no need to distinguish between the two.

There is a lot of hype, bluff and bluster surrounding it, as we all know. And those 'in

> ***"In five years' time there won't be any internet companies – because all businesses will be internet businesses"***
> Andy Grove
> Chairman
> Intel Corporation

the know' appear to inhabit a totally different planet to others who have yet to grasp the nettle and find out what all the fuss is about.

Cutting through the guff and the 'nerd speak', serious business people now agree that e-business is re-making the business world by:

- Affecting virtually every business process and function
- Changing conventional concepts and rules about strategic alliances, outsourcing, competition, industry specialisation and customer relationships
- Creating a wealth of information about customers, enabling businesses to anticipate and satisfy individual needs with pinpoint precision.
- Dissolving the lines between industries
- Challenging every organisation to think about the way it does business.

Serious commentators say that it is important to recognise how truly different e-business is from any other development of our time. Everything that has gone before it has eventually become obsolete, but the gurus argue that e-business is just the opposite. This time *users* will be rendered obsolete if they don't run fast or hard enough to utilise the new capabilities e-business delivers. That's fighting talk . . . but how's all this going to happen?

The mass migration to an e-business model will occur in stages, predict the tecchie soothsayers. Some companies have already moved well beyond the first stage – establishing an internet presence or channel – and they are now actively integrating and connecting the buying and selling processes of their web site into back office, customer and marketing systems.

In the next stage, web capabilities are actively integrated throughout the value chain. Here, customers and suppliers work together to build on-line value chains that provide service and reduce costs.

In the final stages, business of all kinds will converge electronically to combine their expertise and provide packaged services. They will push the edge of their current e-business capabilities to transform their strategies, organisations, processes and systems so that they can better meet the needs of their customers. The focus at this stage is on building trust.

When all this comes about, the boundaries between industries will begin to disappear. Companies will un-bundle their operations and retain only those critical to their market position. Cross-industry value chains will come together to create networked organisations and markets.

E-business is an unstoppable, epoch-making idea. Very soon, the name for e-business is likely to be: business.

Big breaker 3: competition for the best people

The most intense battle in business today is not for capital or advanced technology, or market share. It is for talent.

Human resources gurus have been telling us for some time of new attitudes in the workforce toward what is now labelled 'work/life balance'. Survey after survey confirms that employees now want to temper their ambitions for professional achievement and material reward with greater attention to interests away from the job.

This work/life adjustment is the reflection of a deeper shift; an insistence upon defining your own life, priorities and choices to a far greater degree than we have ever seen before.

Rejecting the old corporate ways, today's employees have a passion for autonomy – a belief that given appropriate training and experience and provided with substantial latitude – they will make decisions that enhance the value of the company whilst advancing their own interests.

So far, so good. But hold on, because only the most far-sighted organisations have cottoned-on to the fact that the employer/employee relationship has become *the most important* of all customer/supplier relationships. In a tight labour market, where everyone is looking for talent and innovative thinking, the level of intimacy and personalisation of the customer/supplier relationship is becoming the decisive factor.

Richard Branson's Virgin Atlantic is one such trailblazer. 'People *are* an organisation,' says Richard. 'A company has to adapt to what its people want to do, otherwise it will lose them. It's not easy for management, but where we have done it [at Virgin Atlantic] we've even saved money. Our people are more committed, we have less absenteeism and there's more give and take on both sides.'

The degree to which the employer recognises that each of his (her) people is unique will substantially determine that organisation's fortunes in the competition for the talent they need.

Accepting the new culture and adapting to the new employer/employee relationship will help to attract talent, but it won't guarantee that they will stay. The 'hip' employer of the Millennium must provide its talent with the opportunity for both wealth creation and knowledge.

The rub, of course, is that the more employees earn, and the more they know, the more independent and mobile they become – and the more attractive they are to other potential employers. What a conundrum!

On the flip side, employees provide knowledge to the employer about their education, training, experience, skills, learning, development needs and lifestyle choices. And with this information, the organisation can improve the personalisation of its relationship with employees – keeping it brimming with reward and opportunity.

It can show that it cares for the autonomy of its people, and stay in touch with the market place and new talent. This is no easy juggling act. It requires a combination of powerful technology, coupled with the application of the knowledge gained, and a recognition that traditional employment cultures – and the laws that support them – are becoming as outdated as the ones that sent children and ponies down the coalmines.

Big breaker 4: capitalising on the 'knowledge' economy

We all know that business is about products and services, and about getting them to customers at a sensible profit. But this model doesn't do justice to the pivotal role that *knowledge* has always played, to say nothing about the fact that knowledge is now *the* most valuable business asset.

The world economy has shifted away from traditional assets towards intellectual assets – you and me. Recent statistics say that 75% of the world's corporate market value resides today in intellectual resources.

That explains why companies are increasingly judged by their knowledge assets and their use of those assets to create value.

But we only now learning to identify the types of knowledge which, taken together, represent a dominant asset and an organisation's competitive advantage. Improved communications technology has made the task of communicating with an organisation's people far easier.

The difficulty lies in providing *relevant* material that connects the top, bottom, middle and the furthest reaches of the organisations so that knowledge can be shared quickly, thoroughly and productively. There's massive potential for 'information' overload, crossed signals . . . . and everyone communicating with everyone at the same time.

> ***"What you know, and how quickly you can respond is the key to managing change"***
> Shaun Orpen
> Marketing Director
> Microsoft

Today, many organisations are hell-bent on implementing formal knowledge management (KM) initiatives such as enterprise portals and intranets for sharing knowledge internally, and extranets for sharing knowledge directly with clients and other external stakeholders. It needs a powerful mix of focus, planning, technology and especially education to make it work. But those who do will put themselves miles in front of competitors with less drive.

Doing it well invariably means support from the top, with the Chief Executive Officer vigorously articulating the knowledge management vision and demonstrating its importance to the organisation's ultimate goal . . . the creation of greater shareholder value, increased profit, better business, etc.

So, KM initiatives are not simply a bolt on. They must be tied to specific business issues or strategy and funded for the long haul. Deep pockets may be needed to a create system which will share and harvest knowledge which will benefit the organisation. The trick is to get the right information to the right folk in the right way. Not easy, but that is the challenge facing the knowledge economy.

Big breaker 5: self-empowerment

People are waking up to the realisation that they are more powerful than they ever thought – provided they have the skills and attitudes in demand by those who are willing to pay for them. The advent of the internet has brought a veritable 'gold rush' of talented individuals – many self-taught – into the entrepreneurial arena.

These days one good idea could, indeed, make you a million. No long apprenticeship or working your way through the managerial ranks here; quick wins are the goal many are seeking.

All of this presupposes creativity and talent backed by the will, determination and courage to see a concept through to success. Individuals working in global mega-corporations are no different.

Age and experience count for less than creativity, dynamism and the ability to get things done. But don't take my word for it, talk to those top business leaders in the US and Europe whose views were canvassed for a recent survey on what they looked for in 'fast track' individuals – the kind of people the organisation needed to rely on for its present and future success.

Unsurprisingly, the business leaders named the ability to prioritise, to meet deadlines, to motivate themselves and others, to think 'outside the box' and get things done . . . fast. This book simply picks up on what some of the world's best businesspeople want, and you can meet their needs by *using* the tools presented in these pages.

Your future, whether you work in an organisation, subcontract to it or work alone, has never been more assured – provided you keep up with the changing ways of the world and use your innate skills to keep you head and shoulders above those who do not.

The five 'killer' questions

Am I . . . ?	Yes	No	Maybe
Clear about the megatrends affecting me/my business?			
Responding quickly enough to them?			
Evaluating properly the value of e-business to me and my business?			
Fully capitalising on my knowledge and that of my organisation?			
Happy with my reward versus life balance?			
What am I going to do next?			

Most people are more concerned about what is happening to them today than thinking about the future. Just spending time ruminating about what might happen in the future is the secret of 'visionary' thinking. It can set you aside from your colleagues, or even make your fortune.

Where am I now?

Success Secret No. 5 is to see the 'big picture'. It means taking a wider view if what is happening now and looks set to happen in the future, and assessing its implications for you and the business you are in.

Some trends will produce massive opportunities – if you 'see' them. Others could threaten to make you, your role or your business extinct. Envisioning the future, indeed creating it, is the mark of great people and organisations. It is at the same time both a predatory and a protective strategy.

All entrepreneurs know that there's money to be made in emerging trends, but they are also acutely aware that good things don't last forever, and their ability to succeed lies in knowing when to move from an 'out of favour' sector to the next latest thing.

The five megatrends here are the ones I see as important just now. From your perspective you may see others. What do they tell you about what your next big move should be?

Chapter 16

A final word – just say 'yes'

Organisations are downsizing, delayering and decentralising. They're outsourcing, globalising and consolidating. Their people are hot desking, teleworking and demanding ever more of their employer. They are managing their knowledge, their key relationships and their 'work life balance' like never before.

If all this sounds like management gobbledegook to you, it's not important. What it all adds up to is change – at a pace which none of us have ever seen.

But businesses need people like you to help them stay ahead of the pack. Where are the big ideas, the creativity and innovation going to come from? And who will provide the drive and courage to implement them. On both counts it could be you.

As we've seen throughout this book, to make things happen, to build something better than you already have, you need a passion to do it, mixed with determination and a 'can do' attitude. The great people and organisations throughout history have demonstrated that fact. They've taught us that it doesn't go right every time; there's no foolproof formula for success. In fact, failure has very often been the building block of their achievement.

The real secret of success is their ability to see an opportunity and to breathe life into it, to make that chance their own. When it comes down to it the only real thing stopping each one of us from being like the 'greats' is our attitude to what is possible for us to achieve.

I changed my life around when I finally recognised that my overwhelming workload, coupled with massive pressure to perform, had to be faced and beaten. There was no other choice: I'd either be dead physically – or mentally – through fatigue and exhaustion. The doctors and psychiatrists use the fancy phrase 'executive burn out'.

You may, or may not, feel the same way yourself. It doesn't really matter. What does matter, however, is that you start to use some or all of the easily 'do-able' success and survival strategies in these pages. They are designed to take the pressure off you by giving you tools to perform better and faster – to make you a creator of change, not a victim of it.

Most people would agree that ultimately life is all about having fun and being creative and productive – feeling the buzz and excitement of developing something new, the thrill of success, the energy generated by your enthusiasm to get things done . . . the sheer joy of achieving your goals. It's about carving out time; time for your loved ones, time for yourself, time to contribute something back.

This isn't 'woolly-headed' thinking, a pipe dream that simply won't happen. It could be your life. It all hinges on using the techniques designed to allow you to emulate the way great individuals and organisations work. They move fast, they test and experiment, make quick decisions, tolerate failure and applaud success. They focus on what's important and, above all, they commit themselves to do it.

Walking barefoot on broken glass is now relatively easy for me. What one scared me to death has become second nature. I've applied the techniques in this book to overcome my own fear of failure, of looking foolish and of 'having a go' at something that is outside my comfort zone.

Occasionally when I'm demonstrating the feat a shard of glass will cut me – a timely reminder, I think, that everything we do has some element of risk to it. The knack is to focus on what you are doing, and what you want to achieve, whilst respecting the risks you take. Respecting the risk doesn't mean you should let it stop you 'just doing it'.

Every day we are making decisions to do, or not do, something. Too many times we say 'no' when we could say 'yes'. The chance to achieve what you want to do is waiting; you have the tools to do it. What you do next is up to you. Just say yes!

> *Our deepest fear is not that we are inadequate.*
>
> *Our deepest fear is that we are powerful beyond measure. It is our light, not our darkness, that most frightens us.*
>
> *We ask ourselves, 'Who am I to be brilliant, gorgeous, talented and fabulous?' Actually, who are you not to be?*
>
> *Your playing small doesn't serve the world. There is nothing enlightening about shrinking so that other people won't feel insecure around you.*
>
> *And, as we let our own light shine, we unconsciously give other people permission to do the same.*
>
> *As we are liberated from our own fear, our presence automatically liberates others.*
>
> Nelson Mandela
> *1994 Inaugural Speech*

Explore some more – further reading and sources of info

So you've read the book, picked up a few tips and ideas you can implement straight away, and, hopefully, had your appetite whetted to discover more in the areas that have really grabbed your attention. One of the key messages of the book is the importance of taking action before the impetus to 'do something' dissipates.

You can choose to use the knowledge you've gained as a spur to action, or not, it's your choice. As a starter why not visit the Barefoot website at **www.barefootbook.com**. It's full of self-tests and exercises designed to give you ideas on how you can be more creative, techniques to help you define and reach your goals, extra material that it wasn't possible to squeeze into a concise book like this and, of course, a demonstration of me walking barefoot on broken glass.

You'll also find references to other Capstone books dealing in more detail with some of the issues highlighted here. Check out, for example:

- *A Freethinker's A–Z of the New World of Business*, by Stuart Crainer, Bruce Tulgan and Watts Wacker

An eclectic and encyclopaedic guide to the people, concepts and innovations which are shaping business, society and work today.

- *?WHAT IF! How to Start a Creative Revolution at Work*, by Dave Allan, Matt Kingdom, Kris Murrin and Daz Rudkin
This one delivers powerful insights that demolish the myths of creativity and help you not just change the way you think but change the way you do things.
- *The Knowledge Advantage*, by Rudy Ruggles and Dan Holtshouse
Gives solid advice on how to turn knowledge into products, how to use it for powerful strategic decisions and, most important, how to profit from the knowledge you and your people have.
- *Blur . . . The Speed of Change in the Connected Economy*, by Stan Davis and Christopher Meyer
Traditional boundaries between products and services, and industries are breaking down at a phenomenal rate. How will it affect you and your sector? This book gives an insight from consultants who are making it happen.

There's lots more references to great works in the further reading section below as well. Have a skim read and see if any catch your eye.

Further reading

Bandler, R., *Using Your Brain – For a Change* (Real People Press, 1997).

Benson, Herbert, *The Relaxation Response* (William Morrow, 1975).

Black, Jack, *Mindstore: The Ultimate Mental Fitness Programme* (Thorsons, 1994).

Black, Roger, *Getting Things Done* (Michael Joseph, 1987).

Blanchard, Kenneth, William Oncken Jr and Hal Burrows, *The One Minute Manager Meets the Monkey* (Fontana/Collins, 1990).

Bliss, Edwin C., *Doing It Now* (Macdonald, 1983).

Buzan, Tony, *Use Your Memory* (BBC Publications, 1986).

Calano, Jimmy and Jeff Salzman, *Career Tracking: 26 Success Shortcuts to the Top* (Gower, 1988).

Carlzon, Jan, *Moments of Truth* (Ballinger, 1987).

Carnegie, Dale, *How to Stop Worrying and Start Living* (Cedar Books, 1962).

Collins, James C. and Jerry I. Porras, *Built to Last: Successful Habits of Visionary Companies* (Century Business Books, 1996).

Covey, Steven R., *The Seven Habits of Highly Effective People*.

Cutler, Wade E., *Triple Your Reading Speed* (Arco, 1970).

Doyle, Michael and David Strauss, *How to Make Meetings Work* (Berkley Publishing Group, 1976).

Drucker, Peter, *The Effective Executive* (Harper & Row, 1966).

Dyer, Wayne, *Your Erroneous Zones* (Sphere, 1977).

Feldman, Mark L. and Michael F. Spratt, *Five Frogs on a Log – a CEO's Field Guide to Accelerating the Transition in Mergers, Acquisitions, and Gut Wrenching Change* (Harper Business, 1999).

Gallwey, W. Timothy, *The Inner Game of Golf* (Random House, 1986).

Gawain, Shakti, *Creative Visualisation* (Bantam Books, 1978).

Gibson, Rowan, *Rethinking the Future* (Nicholas Brearley Publishing, 1998).

Hancock, Jonathan, *Mindpower System: A Step by Step Guide to Improving your Memory* (Hodder & Stoughton, 1995).

Hill, Napoleon and W. Clement Stone, *Success Through a Positive Mental Attitude* (Prentice Hall, 1960).

Hill, Napoleon, *Think and Grow Rich* (Fawcett Crest, 1983)

Jeffers, Susan, *End the Struggle and Dance With Life: How to Build Yourself Up when the World Gets You Down* (Coronet Books, 1996).

Jenkins, Sarah, *Trying to be Human: Zen Talks from Cheri Huber* (Present Perfect Books, 1995).

Joseph, Arthur Samuel, *The Sound of the Soul* (Health Communications, 1996).

Lorayne, Harry, *How to Develop a Super Power Memory* (A. Thomas, 1967).

Lorayne, Harry, *Memory Makes Money* (Thorsons, 1990).

Maltz, Maxwell, *Psycho Cybernetics* (Thorsons, 1969).

Maslow, Abraham, *The Farther Reaches of Human Nature* (Penguin, 1976).

McCormack, Mark H., *What They Don't Teach You at Harvard Business School* (Collins, 1984).

McWilliams, John-Roger and Peter McWilliams, *Do it! Let's Get Off Our Buts* (Prelude Press, 1991).

Nacson, Leon and Deepak Chopra, *How to Live in a World of Infinite Possibilities* (Random House, 1998).

O'Keefe, John, *Your One Week Way to Mind Fitness* (Thorsons, 1994).

Page, Michael, *Visualisation: The Key to Fulfilment* (Aquarian Press, 1990).

Pedler, Mike and Tom Boydell, *Managing Yourself* (Fontana, 1989).

Peters, Tom, *Thriving on Chaos* (Alfred A. Knopf, 1982).

PricewaterhouseCoopers, *The Innovation Survey* (1999).

Robbins, Anthony, *Unlimited Power* (Simon & Schuster, 1997).

Rosenfield, Israel, *The Invention of Memory: A New View of the Brain* (Basic Books, 1988).

Shapiro, Mo, *Understanding Neuro-Linguistic Programming*. The Institute of Management Foundation (Hodder & Stoughton, 1998).

Thompson, Charles 'Chic', *What a Great Idea: Key Steps Creative People Take* (Harper Perennial, 1992).

Von Oech, Roger, *A Whack on the Side of the Head* (Thorsons, 1990)

Wilde, Stuart, *The Secrets of Life* (White Dove International, 1990).

Wright, Andrew, *How to Improve your Mind* (Cambridge University Press, 1987).

Index